CW00525937

Berlitz®

BAKU
POCKET GUIDE

Walking Eye
mobile app

Discover the world's best destinations with the Insight Guides Walking Eye app, available to download for free in the App Store and Google Play.

The container app provides easy access to fantastic free content on events and activities taking place in your current location or chosen destination, with the possibility of booking, as well as the regularly-updated Insight Guides travel blog: Inspire Me. In addition, you can purchase curated, premium destination guides through the app, which feature local highlights, hotel, bar, restaurant and shopping listings, an A to Z of practical information and more. Or purchase and download Insight Guides eBooks straight to your device.

TOP 10 ATTRACTIONS

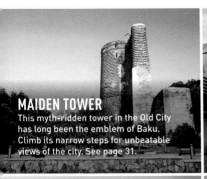

MAIDEN TOWER
This myth-ridden tower in the Old City has long been the emblem of Baku. Climb its narrow steps for unbeatable views of the city. See page 31.

AZERBAIJAN CARPET MUSEUM
Thousands of carpets and traditional garments fill this museum. See page 46.

BOULEVARD
The leafy promenade, lined with cafes and benches, has been the stomping ground of Bakuvians for over a century. See page 39.

ATESHGAH OF BAKU
A holy site in Surakhani and a symbol of Azerbaijan's deep-rooted Zoroastrian past. See page 75.

FOUNTAINS SQUARE
A vibrant piazza and a popular meeting point, with a wealth of restaurants, cafes and shops. See page 52.

NATIONAL MUSEUM OF AZERBAIJAN LITERATURE
This statue-engraved literature museum honours the country's most famed poet, Nizami Ganjavi. See page 54.

FLAME TOWERS
A nod to Azerbaijan's moniker of 'land of fire', this trio of flame-shaped skyscrapers are covered in thousands of LED screens that light up the city at night. See page 62.

SHIRVANSHAH'S PALACE
A sprawling, religious complex once home to the Shirvan dynasty of the Middle Ages. See page 33.

GOBUSTAN NATIONAL PARK
This arid, vast expanse is home to thousands of prehistoric petroglyphs and over half of the world's mud volcanoes. See page 72.

HEYDAR ALIYEV CENTER
Architecture lovers rejoice: this masterpiece has become a symbol of 21st century Baku. See page 69.

A PERFECT DAY

8.00am

Breakfast
Enjoy a leisurely breakfast at your hotel or head to one of the restaurants in the Old City, like Sehrli Tendir, for something more traditional. Breakfast here usually consists of bread, local cheese, honey, jam and black tea.

10.00am

Old Baku
Start by climbing the steep steps of the Maiden Tower for panoramic views of Baku and its crescent-shaped harbour. From here, wander inside the 12th-century walls to explore Shirvanshah's Palace, a sprawling religious complex dating back to the Middle Ages.

11.30am

Tea break
There isn't much Bakuvians love more than tea. Take a break from strolling the Old City's cobbled alleys and head to Cay Bagi 145 on Kichik Gala (just behind Maiden Tower) for a samovar of black tea and *paxlava*. Skip the sugar and drink your tea with a spoonful of *mürabba*, a local fruit preserve available in a variety of flavours.

12.30pm

Books and art
After ducking in and out of colourful bazaars (and maybe trying your hand at haggling for a rug or two), walk further down Kichik Gala Street to peek inside local artist Ali Shamsi's colourful studio. Then, continue down to the Museum of Miniature Books, home to thousands of minuscule volumes.

2.00pm

Lunch
Walk to the boulevard for lunch at the legendary café Mirvari (see page 111). Get a table under its Sydney Opera House-esque canopy and order from the long menu of local salads and kebabs. Then, visit the Azerbaijan Carpet Museum to learn about the country's impenetrable love affair with carpets.

IN BAKU

6.00pm

Take in the city view
Walk back down to Neftchilar Avenue and get the funicular from Shovkat Alakbarova street up to the Flame Towers and Highland Park, the highest point in the city, for unbeatable views over Baku.

10.00pm

After dinner drinks
The cool kids of Baku aren't big on nightclubs. Instead, spend the evening sipping a drink on the boulevard or head back to Fountains Square to the arty ROOM wine bar, which serves up a good selection of local and international wines, often has live jazz performances and stays open until 4am.

4.00pm

Go downtown
Walk towards Fountains Square, a buzzy piazza with shops, restaurants and bars, and amble the adjoining, chandelier-lined Nizami Street. Stop to admire the nearby statue-engraved façade of the National Museum of Azerbaijani Literature and people-watch in the lush gardens opposite.

7.30pm

Dinner
Come back down to the Old City to enjoy a traditional dinner at the caravanserai-turned-restaurant Mugam Club, accompanied by a live performance of the country's melancholic musical genre. The *qutab* and *sabzi plov* here are exceptionally tasty.

CONTENTS

INTRODUCTION

For the most part, Baku is a city reborn. In the last decade, rapid gentrification has been forging changes in the once obscure Azerbaijani capital at a pace that has astonished even Bakuvians. Yet at its core remains the tradition-soaked Old City (İçəri Şəhər), a 12th-century, fortressed neighbourhood that comprised Baku before the city's metamorphic, oil boom expansion. Step outside the walls and you'll see a wealth of Baroque mansions of oil barons past, lots of clean, leafy parks, and spanking new architectural marvels, like the gargantuan Flame Towers that dwarf the city's once ubiquitous, timeworn Soviet mass housing. Its rebirth has also introduced a swarm of new restaurants, hotels and an improved public transport system, however it remains considerably cheaper than most European cities.

The cultural, artsy scene is having a moment too; an old navy base has been converted into an art centre, the old-school jazz scene of the 60s and 70s is witnessing a renaissance, and funding is being pumped into the city's dusty outlying attractions to promote its Palaeolithic and Zoroastrian past. Whatever your reason for visiting Baku, it only takes a quick stroll through its streets to realise that no other city manages, quite so visually and potently, to be both Asian and European, both modern and traditional. It's that culmination of ancient, Silk Road-era troves, blindingly shiny architecture and a desert-ringed hinterland that makes Baku such a compelling metropolis.

GEOGRAPHY AND POPULATION

Azerbaijan is a mostly mountainous country in the Caucasus region, and is around a third of the size of the UK. It shares its borders with Russia to the north, Iran to the south, Georgia to the northwest and Armenia to the west, with the Caspian Sea coastline to the east. Via the Azerbaijani exclave of Nakhchivan in the southwest, there's also a small border with Turkey, only 15km (9 miles) long. Its capital, Baku, is the largest in the Caucasus, sprawling 2,130 sq km (822 sq miles) around the southern shore of the beak-shaped, semi-arid Absheron Peninsula.

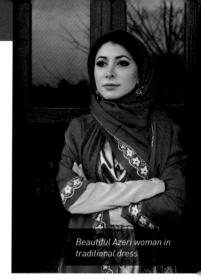

Beautiful Azeri woman in traditional dress

In 2019, the country's population reached 10 million, 2.2 million of whom live in Baku. The vast majority (over 90 percent) of those living in Baku are ethnically Azerbaijani, with the rest mostly made up of Russians, Lezgis (an ethnic group from northeastern Azerbaijan), Jews and a small number of other ethnic minorities. The port city's story first began in 1191, when an earthquake destroyed the region's former capital, the seismic city of Shamakhi, and rulers of the Shirvan dynasty moved their governing seat to Baku.

At 28 metres (92ft) below sea level, it's the lowest lying capital city in the world and experiences a semi-arid climate with dry, hot summers, and mild, occasionally wet winters. The name Baku is said to derive from the Persian 'bad kube', meaning 'city of winds', which, thanks to the year-round strong gales from the Caspian Sea, has gone on to become the city's moniker. The topography of Baku is vastly different and varied as you head out of the city centre — take Gobustan National Park, a stretch of rocky, arid land, home to ancient petroglyphs and bubbling mud volcanoes; or the traditional villages, with mysterious wonders like the eternally burning hillside of Yanar Dag, the origin of the Azerbaijan appellation, 'land of fire'; and the vast, fauna-rich Absheron National Park, sprawled across the very tip of the peninsula.

BAKUVIANS

Azerbaijanis, or Azeris for short, belong to the Turkic ethnic group and speak Azerbaijani, a language most similar to

⊘ THE CASPIAN SEA

Despite its sea status, the Caspian Sea is actually the largest lake in the world as it doesn't feed into another body of water and is landlocked. Azerbaijan's coastline stretches for roughly 825km (513 miles), while the crescent-shaped Bay of Baku in the city centre occupies 20 kilometres (12.5 miles). The sea is shared with Kazakhstan and Turkmenistan to the east, Iran to the south and Russia to the north.

Its name derives from the ancient Kaspi people who inhabited Transcaucasia, which roughly corresponds to modern-day Azerbaijan, Georgia and Armenia. Its most prized produce is Beluga caviar, extracted from the sturgeons abundant in these waters. The price of Azerbaijani Beluga caviar, which you can find in specialist shops and markets around Baku, has risen significantly since the Soviet Union's collapse, when it was a staple in most Azerbaijani households, and today costs around 150 AZN (£71) per jar.

For a beach day, there are a number of clean, public beaches around Baku's Caspian coast, the most popular being Bilgah in the northeast.

Turkish. Many of those living in Baku also speak Russian, and a number of the younger generation speak English, too. The majority of Bakuvians have a no-rush, laid-back attitude, and can spend hours aimlessly gossiping, eating and strolling the boulevard. In the Old City, you will find them whiling away time on rug-laden pavements, playing backgammon or dominoes, and sipping tea into the night.

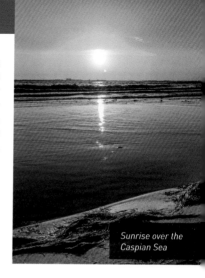

Sunrise over the Caspian Sea

On the boulevard – they're mostly rollerskating, jogging, and, come night-time, dressed up to the nines to walk hand in hand until the early hours. Most Azeris are warm and hospitable, and will often show their love by opening their doors to visitors and dishing up superabundant, home-cooked food — don't pass up the chance to eat in somebody's home if you get an offer. Just remember not to sit on the corner of the table, as, according to local superstition, this will hinder your chances of getting married, something very important in local culture.

ARCHITECTURE

Multi-faceted Baku is filled with a cocktail of outlandish architecture ranging from the 12th century to the present day. Take the all-consuming Flame Towers, the tallest being 182m (597ft), that light up the city with 10,000 LED-powered screens every night. In its forefront is the ancient, placid,

The alphabet

The Azerbaijani alphabet is Latin and almost identical to Turkish. Distinctive letters include 'ə', which is pronounced like the 'a' in 'back', ç is ch, c is j, ğ is a gargled g, q sounds like a hard g, ş is sh, and the undotted ı grunted. The letter x sounds like nothing in the English language, and w doesn't exist.

Old City, where the myth-fuelled Maiden Tower and Shirvanshah's Palace, once home to Baku's rulers of the Middle Ages, sit majestically among centuries-old mosques, hammams and rug shops, happy in the knowledge that this will always, according to locals, be 'the real Baku'.

In the east, the meringue-like curves of the abstract Heydar Aliyev Center, by Zaha Hadid, softened the area's backdrop of monotonous Soviet-era housing when it was completed in 2012. On the boulevard, you'll find the impressive Azerbaijan Carpet Museum, shaped, quite impressively, like a giant roll of gold carpet. Dimly-lit Baroque mansions line Nizami Street in downtown Baku, providing the city with a romantic, Parisian flair, yet further down on Neftchilar Avenue, the ogive-arched Government House, or Dom Soviet, is an imposing reminder of Baku's austere, Soviet-era past.

RENAISSANCE OF BAKU

Baku has undergone several transformations: when it first became the capital in the 12th century, followed by the oil boom of the 19th century, then its pivotal Soviet era, and most recently, the transformative, money-fuelled 2000s. Before the dawn of the millennium, unless they worked for BP or had family here, those in the west probably didn't know much about Baku. The immediate years following the dissolution of the Soviet Union were confusing, as the city, and country, tried to re-emerge on its own two feet, figuring out what it meant to be 'Azeri'. Gradually, culture, music, TV, media, language, religion and traditions were shed of their Russian influences, and Baku witnessed another oil boom in 2005. But nothing has propelled it to such international recognition as entering the Eurovision Song Contest for the first time in 2008, winning it in 2011, and subsequently hosting it in the climactic 2012 — the most expensive Eurovision to date — which left spectators asking, 'Where is Azerbaijan?'

The years that followed saw Baku launch the inaugural European Games in 2015, become a Formula 1 host city in 2017 and host the UEFA Europa League final in 2019. Regeneration even reached entire neighbourhoods, like Sovetski, a historic district that was bulldozed in favour of the verdant Central Park, which opened in the spring of 2019. Despite the turbo-modernisation, the city refuses to renounce its humble ways. Head to the Old City or the outlying neighbourhoods to find old men in aerodrome hats fondling prayer beads, grannies in paisley headscarves making bread on the side of the road, and rusty, decades old Ladas groaning their way through narrow alleyways. On the surface, Baku has changed, but its old-world charm certainly remains.

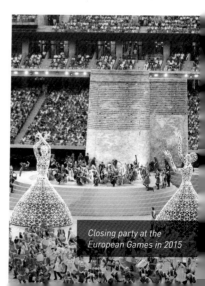

Closing party at the European Games in 2015

A BRIEF HISTORY

Baku's beginning has historians scratching their heads. It can't be pinpointed exactly when civilisation reached here, but the weird and wonderful petroglyphs in nearby Gobustan National Park, said to date back some 40,000 years, suggest that it was around the Palaeotholic age. Gobustan, a vast, arid expanse southwest of Baku, is home to over 6,000 oddball sketches depicting the norms of daily life a millennia ago. It was these scribbles, in particular the one of a reed boat, that convinced Norwegian explorer Thor Heyerdahl that Azerbaijan must have been the home of early civilisation and his ancestors, the Vikings, who used the same style of sea transportation. The very first human settlers in this territory are believed to be those from Caucasian Albania, the ancient name of modern-day Azerbaijan. Caucasian Albanians, who bore no ethnic or geographical link to contemporary Albania, lived in this pocket of the Caucasus from the 3rd century BC until the 8th century AD.

The name 'Baku' is believed to derive from the Persian 'bad kube', meaning 'the city of winds', or the ancient Caucasian word 'bak', meaning sun or God. A Latin inscription at the bottom of Boyuk Dash mountain (Böyük Daş) in Gobustan National Park suggests that Romans were present here sometime between AD 84 and 96. Ramana, an ancient village east of Baku on the Absheron Peninsula, also strengthens this theory, with sources likening its name to 'Romana'.

Through time, whether for its ideal location by the sea or the revolutionary discovery of oil, the city has been lusted after and conquered by multiple empires, from the Mongols to the Persians, and, most recently, the Russians. For seven decades of the 20th century, the country bent to the will of the Soviets, causing an all-consuming effect on its culture. It wasn't until 1991 that this nation with a wildly tangled and convoluted past learned how to be independent.

ZOROASTRIANISM

The ancient, fire-worshipping religion of Zoroastrianism, one of the world's oldest monotheist religions, was founded by Prophet Zoroaster and became predominant in Azerbaijan as early as the first millennium BC, lending the country its nickname, the 'land of fire'. Legends believe that Prophet Zoroaster was born in the state of Caucasian Albania, also known as Arran, an ancient state split between a section of modern-day Azerbaijan and a small area of Dagestan in southern Russia.

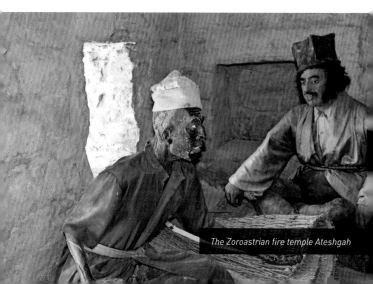

The Zoroastrian fire temple Ateshgah

The great Silk Road

Baku's position by the Caspian Sea made it one of the key transit points during the great Silk Road era between the 2nd and 15th century. Boats carrying goods from Asia would use the port of Baku to cross over into Europe.

Caucasian Albanians, who resided here until the 8th century, converted to Zoroastrianism during the Persian dynasties, until the Muslims conquered Persia in the 7th century, leading to the religion's gradual, inevitable demise. Ateshgah of Baku, a Zoroastrian fire temple in the village of Suraxani in the east of the city, acted as a worshipping temple for Zoroastrians, Hindus and Sikhs through different times. Although most Zoroastrians fled to India after the arrival of Islam, both Ateshgah and the eternally-burning hillside of nearby Yanar Dag still attracts believers who come here to pray.

SHIRVAN AND SAFAVID DYNASTIES

The story of Baku as a powerhouse of the Caucasus started in the late 9th century, when the historic region of Shirvan, now modern-day Azerbaijan, was governed by the Shirvanshahs from the late 9th century through to the early 16th century. After an earthquake devastated the city of Shamakhi in 1191, ruler Shirvanshah Ahistan I moved the dynasty's capital to Baku. He built several mosques and started laying the foundations of Shirvanshah's Palace, which still stands in the Old City today.

The next prominent leader was Ibrahim I (1382–1417), who ordered the reconstruction of the city walls after the Mongols rampaged through Baku in the 13th century. Shirvanshah Khalilullah I (1417–62), son of Ibrahim I, gave Baku a new breath of life after he completed the construction of Shirvanshah's Palace.

In 1501, Baku fell into the hands of Shah Ismail, poet and founder of the Persian Safavid dynasty, who went on to rule here from 1501 to 1722. The Safavids, who are considered to be among the most defining rulers of Iran, forcibly converted Baku from Sunni to Shia Islam, and made Tabriz, in northern Iran, their capital.

In 1517, the Ottoman Empire invaded Baku, but it returned to Safavid rule again in 1607. Khatai, a raion (district) in the east of Baku, is named in honour of the leader, as this is the name he used to pen his poems. He is credited as being the first person to use the Azerbaijani language on a state level, and in 1993, a monument in his honour was built in Baku. For the next century or so, power over Baku shifted back and forth between the Ottomans and Persians.

RUSSIAN EMPIRE AND OIL BOOM

In 1723, Baku was captured by the imperial Russians. Czar Peter the Great set his eyes on Baku's bound-less oil resources, which were already providing the Persians with an impres-sive income. He believed that taking control of Baku and its oil would strengthen Russia's trade relations between the East and Europe. Nicknamed 'black gold', oil had been noted here as early as the

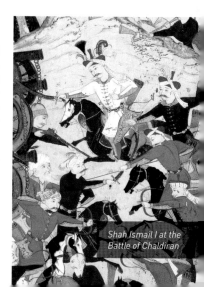

Shah Ismail I at the Battle of Chaldiran

A train of tankers carrying oil from the Nobel Brothers oil wells

10th century, and in 1846, the world's first oil well was dug in Bibi-Heybat, just south of Baku city centre. But it wasn't until 1872, when the Russians lifted the commercial regulations of oil, that it propelled the city to new heights and made it a global frontrunner of the oil and gas industry.

Investors became millionaires overnight just by digging up the earth in their plots of land. This attracted thousands of investors to the city, and lavish mansions of oil barons started sprouting by the Caspian Sea. The most prominent baron was Haji Zeynalabdin Taghiyev, an Azeri bricklayer who discovered gold in his land in Bibi-Heybat. Taghiyev, who was given the nickname 'Father of the Nation', became one of the city's greatest figures by using his oil-funded wealth to invest in Azerbaijan's economy, from wine-making and fisheries to the Baku-Shollar water pipeline and opening the first girls' boarding school in the Caucasus.

The population of Baku, which was less than 10,000 when conquered by the Russians in the 18th century, rose to approximately a quarter of a million by the beginning of World War I as the city expanded out of its original, fortress walls. In his 1905 book, *Baku: An Eventful History,* British author J.D. Henry wrote: 'Baku is greater than any other oil city in the world. If oil is king, Baku is its throne.' That's because by the early 20th century, Azerbaijan was responsible for supplying half of the world's oil. By 1941, it's reported that oil extraction reached a stupendous 23.6 million tonnes, which went on to play an important role in the Soviet Union's victory in World War II. 1949 saw the construction of 'Oil Rocks' (Neft Daşları), the world's first offshore oil platform out at sea, approximately 90km (60 miles) from Baku. From here on, Azerbaijan's offshore oil industry continued to grow, with the development of offshore oil exploration and extraction, and offshore oil rigs soon became synonymous with the Baku coastline.

⊙ NOBEL BROTHERS IN BAKU

In 1874, Swedish-born Robert Nobel, of the Nobel brothers, realised the commercial possibilities of oil in Baku and purchased a refinery here. Five years later, Robert and his brothers, Alfred and Ludwig, went on to create one of the largest oil companies in the world, Branobel. A significant chunk of Alfred's will came from Azerbaijani oil earnings, which then went on to fund the coveted Nobel Peace Prize.

Villa Petrolea, a verdant residential suburb built for employees of the company, is now home to the Nobel Brothers House Museum in Baku's Keshla district. Lev Landau, a well-known Soviet physicist born in Baku, went on to win the Nobel Prize in 1962.

BATTLE OF BAKU

In 1918, Azerbaijan joined the short-lived Transcaucasian Republic along with Georgia and Armenia, but this dissolved after just one month. On 28 May 1918, the country enjoyed a brief, two-year stint of independence and became the first secular democratic nation in the Muslim world. Today, the date is celebrated as a national holiday, and has a metro station and street named in its honour.

After gaining independence from the Russians, the Democratic Republic's government temporarily moved to Ganja, the country's second largest city. This was because of a conflict in Baku between a coalition of Bolsheviks, Dashnaks and Mensheviks, known as the Baku Commune and led by the ethnically Armenian revolutionary Stepan Shaumian, and the Ottoman army, led by Nuri Pasha. The bloody, month-long battle, more commonly known as the Battle of Baku, led to the tactical massacring of Muslim Azeris by the Dashnak Armenian forces, triggering the ethnically charged Azerbaijani-Armenian war.

⊘ A FROZEN CONFLICT

The unresolved Nagorno-Karabakh War was a deadly dispute between Azerbaijan and Armenia over a landlocked exclave in southwestern Azerbaijan. The region lies in Azerbaijan but has an ethnically Armenian population and is backed by Armenia.

Full-blown war first broke out in 1988 when the de facto state voted to join Armenia, but when a truce was signed in 1994, it left Nagorno-Karabakh in Armenian hands. The ethnic strife, which has its roots in the early 20th century, is believed to have cost up to 30,000 lives with hundreds of thousands of people displaced.

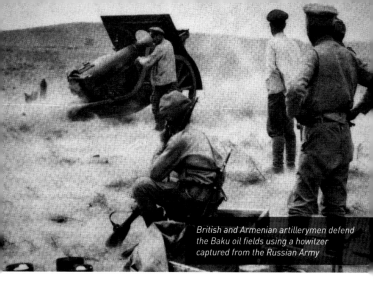

British and Armenian artillerymen defend the Baku oil fields using a howitzer captured from the Russian Army

The coalition soon collapsed, and in September of that year, the Azerbaijanis and the Ottoman Empire stormed Baku and declared it once again the capital of the country.

SOVIETIZATION AND INDEPENDENCE

Azerbaijan became a Socialist Soviet Republic on 28 April 1920 when Baku was invaded by the Red Army of Soviet Russia, and remained a member until its dissolution in 1991. Being a member of the Soviet Union for over 70 years had metamorphic effects on Azerbaijan, significantly reshaping the country's culture, from language and education to religion and housing. Under Soviet rule, the education system switched to the Russian curriculum, and universities were built across the city, including the Azerbaijan Medical University (1930), Azerbaijan State Economic University (1934) and the Azerbaijan University of Languages (1973). Russian became one of the main school subjects, and,

Azerbaijani president Ilham Aliyev

as a result, it's still spoken by many citizens, although its popularity, especially outside of Baku, started declining after the collapse of the Soviet Union.

In 1990, when the Soviet Union was on the verge of collapse, Baku suffered one of its bloodiest massacres. On the night of 19–20 January, citizens took to the streets to protest for independence, but Mikhail Gorbachev ordered tanks and troops to storm the streets of the Azeri capital to ruthlessly kill hundreds of civilian protesters in a bid to suppress the independence movement and maintain control of the profitable, oil-rich country. The bloodshed Baku endured that sombre night, now known as Black January, was the bloodiest crackdown of a Soviet nation's fight for freedom. The official death toll is contested, but Azeri officials say at least 130 civilians were killed and over 700 were wounded. Gorbachev famously quoted that declaring a state of emergency in Baku that January night was 'the biggest mistake of my political career'.

Azerbaijan finally declared independence from the Soviet Union on 30 August 1991, and became a fully independent republic on 18 October 1991, celebrated as Independence Day. Heydar Aliyev, the former leader of the Azerbaijan Communist Party from 1969–82, became the third president of independent Azerbaijan in 1993, after the short-lived leaderships of predecessors Ayaz Mutallibov and Abulfaz Elchibey. He holds legendary status in Azerbaijan, and is still referred to as 'the national leader'. He died in 2003, and was succeeded by his son Ilham Aliyev, who remains president today.

MODERN BAKU

After breaking free from Soviet shackles, it took time for Azerbaijan to rediscover its identity, and for many years it remained a confounding mix of Azeri, Russian and Turkish. Things slowly changed; guilt-ridden Russians started to leave Baku, Russian lessons were removed from the national curriculum, Turkish dominated music and TV, and Azeris looked towards Islam after decades of religious suppression.

In the dawn of the 2000s, the rebirth of Baku truly began; the construction of glistening architecture, expensive shops

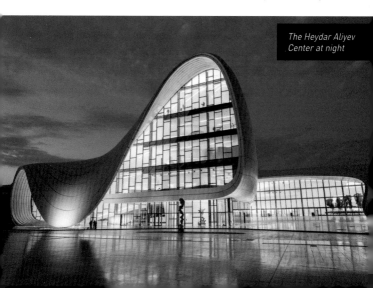

The Heydar Aliyev Center at night

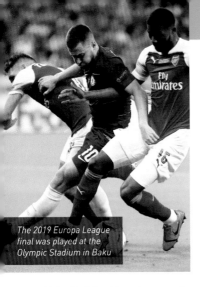

The 2019 Europa League final was played at the Olympic Stadium in Baku

and renovated apartment buildings started to modernise the city's once austere, Soviet backdrop. In 2005, the new oil boom came in the form of the Baku-Tbilisi-Ceyhan pipeline, which started pumping oil from the Caspian Sea to the Mediterranean via Georgia. In the 2010s, spectacular architecture started mushrooming; the gargantuan Flame Towers were built and fast became the city's modern emblem, Zaha Hadid put her stamp on the city with the whirling Heydar Aliyev Center, and the Sydney Opera House-inspired Caspian Seafront Mall, still under construction at the time of writing, became a bulging addition to the once rig-filled coastline of the Caspian Sea.

But perhaps Baku's most pivotal moment was when it won, and consequently hosted, the Eurovision Song Contest in 2012. It propelled the city, and country, to international recognition, and it wasn't long before sporting organisations like UEFA and Formula 1 caught wind of the city's potential as a moneyed host. The city even bid to host the 2016 and 2020 Summer Olympics, although both proved unsuccessful. In May 2019, the UEFA Europa League final between London teams Chelsea and Arsenal was played at the Olympic Stadium in Baku and the city will host group stage matches and quarter-finals for the UEFA Euro 2020 tournament in the summer.

HISTORICAL LANDMARKS

3rd century BC–8th century AD Caucasian Albanians are the first humans to settle in the territory.

7th century Arabs conquer Persia. Zoroastrianism gradually dies out.

12th century Maiden Tower and Old City walls are built, although some historians argue that the Maiden Tower was constructed much earlier.

1191 Baku becomes the capital of the Shirvan dynasty after a catastrophic earthquake in Shamakhi.

1723 Baku is captured by the imperial Russians.

1806 and 1828 Azerbaijan becomes part of the Russian Empire.

1846 The world's first oil well is dug in the Bibi-Heybat area of Baku.

1909 Baku Boulevard is constructed.

1918 Azerbaijan declares independence from the Russian Empire.

1920 The Red Army invade Azerbaijan and the country becomes a Soviet Socialist Republic.

1988 The bloody Nagorno-Karabakh War begins.

1990 Black January: Soviet troops massacre civilians in Baku in a bid to stop Azerbaijan's independence movement.

1991 Azerbaijan declares independence from the Soviet Union.

1993 Heydar Aliyev becomes the third president of Azerbaijan.

1994 A ceasefire is signed, leaving Nagorno-Karabakh in Armenian hands.

2000 The Old City, along with the Maiden Tower and Shirvanshah's Palace, is granted Unesco status. Azerbaijan Airlines launches direct flights between London and Baku.

2003 Heydar Aliyev dies. His son, Ilham Aliyev, is elected president.

2007 Gobustan National Park is granted Unesco status.

2012 Baku hosts the Eurovision Song Contest. Building of the Flame Towers is completed.

2015 The inaugural European Games takes place.

2016 Baku becomes an annual host city of the Formula 1 race.

2017 Azerbaijan introduces a simplified e-visa system for visitors.

2019 The UEFA Europa League final is played at the Olympic Stadium.

2020 Baku is partial host of the UEFA Euro 2020 tournament.

Street in the Old City

WHERE TO GO

Baku's mishmash of neighbourhoods are not as distinct and clear-cut as other cities around the world. The ever-evolving metropolis is divided into 12 raions, but most of the popular attractions, like the Old City, Bulvar and Fountains Square, tend to orient around the crescent-shaped bay of the Caspian Sea and in the north tip of the large, central district of Sabail. Just to its north, the bordering two smaller central districts Nasimi and Yasamal are less busy, but abound with lush parks and bazaars.

Although the city now has a sufficient and affordable public transport system, meandering its ancient and modern streets on foot is the best way of getting to know this multifaceted capital, with large stretches of the centre pedestrianised and perfect for ambling. The duration of your stay depends on how deep you want to dig into the city's roots. A week, give or take a day, is perfect for your first taste; spend a few days taking in the charms of central Baku, a few exploring its outlying attractions like the petroglyph-filled Gobustan and the mysterious burning hillside Yanar Dag, and a few for its weird and wonderful pastimes like dipping yourself in a crude oil bath or being scrubbed senseless in a traditional hammam. Whatever you do, do not rush your time here, that's just not the Baku way.

ICHERI SHEHER (OLD CITY)

Icheri Sheher (www.icherisheher.gov.az) is often called 'the real Baku' by locals. The city's much-treasured, Unesco-listed medieval quarter once served as a key hub for traders of the Silk Road, and while the rest of Baku is in a hurry to modernise, the slow-paced way of life here is going nowhere.

The area was built on a site inhabited since the Palaeolithic times, and is housed inside the beautifully-preserved 12th-century walls with four main entrance points. Abounding with the city's most impressive historical treasures, including the Maiden Tower and Shirvanshah's Palace, you can also expect endless rug shops, caravanserais-turned-restaurants and the city's best traditional boutique hotels (see page 136).

Like most of the buildings here, the houses are made of sandstone, with wooden, chestnut-coloured balconies. The architecture bears influences from various cultures, notably Zoroastrian, Sassanian, Arabic, Persian, Shirvani, Ottoman, and Russian cultures. Before the oil boom of the late 19th century, this is where most Bakuvians lived as the city did not extend far outside of these ancient walls. It wasn't until the expansion

Icheri Sheher

of the city, thanks to oil money, that the name Icheri Sheher, meaning 'Inner City', became the official name of this area.

Today, around 1,300 residents live in Icheri Sheher, and the glass, pyramid-shaped metro station here, formerly called Baksovet, was one of the first five stations in Baku's metro system. Definitely dedicate at least two days for savouring this area slowly; elderly women baking bread on the side of the road, old men playing backgammon on rug-clad ground and Soviet-era cars squeezing through winding, cobbled streets are all just another day in this humble neighbourhood.

MAIDEN TOWER

Dubbed as the original emblem of Baku, the **Maiden Tower** ❶ (Qız Qalası; Tue–Sun 11am–6pm) is a well-preserved cylindrical tower said to date back to the 12th century, but the revered Azerbaijani historian Sara Ashurbeyli believed that the tower's foundations were built sometime between the 4th and 6th centuries. The beloved monument is disputed and riddled in myths, and speculations for its purpose have included a fortress, an observatory and a Zoroastrian worship temple.

One of the many legends surrounding the Maiden Tower is that a maiden, said to be the daughter of the khan of Baku, jumped from the top to her death to avoid marrying a man she didn't love. It's also believed that the tower, which slopes towards the Caspian Sea coast, could have been built to honour the goddess of water, one of the sacred elements of the ancient religion Zoroastrianism (see page 17).

Inside, you will find ancient artefacts and information (available in English) documenting the city's evolution. A trip to Baku is not complete until you have mounted the tower's eight floors of gruelling steps (claustrophobics beware, the staircase is narrow) for panoramic views of the city and the Caspian Sea.

Hajinski Residence

Every year (dates vary, but usually at some point between May and September), the Maiden Tower International Arts Festival takes place here, where artists from all around the world celebrate Baku's most treasured emblem through their work. In the past, installations have included decorated mock-ups of the Maiden Tower, gazelles and pomegranates painted in various national styles. Keep an eye out for other holidays and festivals which often take place around this treasured tower. Right next to the tower is the **Hajinski Residence**, the lavish 1912 home of wealthy Azerbaijani landowner Isa Bey Hajinski, who also owned a kerosene refinery in the Black City (now White City). It's one of the tallest mansions of its period.

Art lovers shouldn't miss **QGallery** (www.qgallery.net; Mon–Fri 10am–7pm, Sat–Sun 10.30am–7pm), also called Qiz Qalasi Art Gallery, which is on Qulle Street a few yards away. Opened by professor Salkhab Mammadov in 1999, the gallery's aim was to support artists in the difficult post-Soviet years, and it is now one of the city's most renowned thanks to its rich collection of paintings and sculptures by Azerbaijani artists. Also on this road is **Bukhara Caravanserai**, a 15th-century caravanserai used by merchants and travellers who passed through Baku from Central Asia, in particular those from Bukhara, the ancient city in Uzbekistan that was another key stop on the Silk Road trade route.

Just behind the Maiden Tower is the **Sirataghli Religious-Architectural Complex**, or Bazar Square, a 12th-century architectural complex that was discovered by accident in the 1960s as the old houses of the area were torn down. Some scientists suggest that the complex belonged to sun worshippers, when they noted that the two doors are located in the east and west, where the sun rises and sets. The excavation also revealed 50 tombs underground.

SHIRVANSHAH'S PALACE

Behind the Maiden Tower is **Shirvanshah's Palace ②** (daily 10am–6pm), a beguiling religious complex on the highest point of the Old City and home to northern Azerbaijan's rulers during the Middle Ages. After a devastating earthquake in 1191, the Shirvan dynasty moved the country's capital from Shamakhi to Baku, and began work on the foundations of the palace.

Unfortunately, none of the inscriptions on the palace itself have survived, but the Arabic writing around the top of the mosque's minaret determine its construction date as 1441.

Set aside an afternoon to explore its main building, Diwankhana (where all the official receptions used to take place), the courtyard, the bath house, the mosque and the mausoleum of

Audio tour

To make the most of the Old City head to the wooden, cylindrical information booth opposite the Maiden Tower to rent an audio set for a self-guided tour (5 AZN). Places of interest, where you can stop and listen to historical information, are signposted with headphones all around the neighbourhood.

scientist Seyid Yahya Bakuvi, which was built in the second half of the 15th century.

The complex was officially designated a museum in 1964 and has undergone several restorations. Many excavations have taken place on this site, and some of the most interesting finds have included underground bath houses and passageways, a 9th-century mosque and the remains of St Bartholomew Church – named after one of Jesus Christ's 12 apostles. Legend has it that he was executed here for attempting to convert the devout fire worshippers of Baku, then Caucasian Albania, into Christians. Inside, there's also a place to try on traditional Azerbaijani dress and have your photo taken against a backdrop of colourful tapestry. Unesco has labelled Shirvanshah's Palace 'one of the pearls of Azerbaijan's architecture'.

A few yards away in front of the complex's Murad gate is **Baylar Mosque ❸**, constructed in 1895 on the site of an older mosque. It entwines local architectural influences with those from the west and east, and underwent significant restoration in 2014–15. It now houses the Sacred Relics exhibition showcasing the Quran from various periods.

KICHIK GALA STREET

This quaint, cobbled street, its name meaning 'small castle', runs parallel to the city's medieval walls, stretching from **Gosha Gala Gapisi ❹** (the Old City's double gates) to the tea hotspot of Cay Bagi 145, and is fringed with places to eat, drink and shop for rugs and Soviet-era memorabilia. Just outside Gosha Gala Gapisi, opposite the Constitutional Court of Azerbaijan, is the leafy **Sabir Bagi**, a garden dedicated to satirical poet Mirza Alakbar Sabir. Through the gates, the rug-ridden Sehrli Tendir (see page 110) is outstanding if you're after a typical, Azerbaijani breakfast to kickstart your day.

Further along, duck into **Ali Shamsi Studio** (www.ali-shamsi.com; daily 10am–8pm), home to artist Ali's quirky and rare paintings and art installations. There is a mural of a lion with luminous eyes outside his studio, which is a hit with camera-happy passers-by, and so is the red-lipped woman painted onto the tree opposite.

Down a little side street on the left is the **Museum of Miniature Books** ❺ (Miniatur Kitab Muzeyii; 1 Gala Lane; tel: 12-492 9464; www.minibooks.az; Tue, Wed, Fri–Sun 11am–5pm; free but donations encouraged), home to over 5,000 tiny books, including one that's a nanoscopic 0.75mm by 0.75mm. The collection was curated by the founder, Zarifa Salahova, and the museum is the only one of its kind in the world.

Further down on Kichik Gala Street, tucked into a narrow alleyway through a set of greeny-brown wooden doors, is the winsome **Baku Marionette Theatre** (20 Muslim Magomayev Street; tel: 12-505 6580; www.marionet.az; open seasonally, performances every Sat), founded by artist Tarlan Gorchu, where it's worth catching a soulful performance of Leyli and Majnun, Azerbaijan's answer to Romeo and Juliet. Don't worry about the show being in Azerbaijani – the storyline is fairly easy to follow.

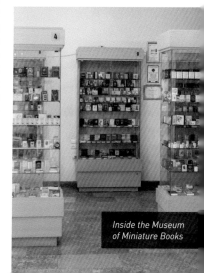

Inside the Museum of Miniature Books

Roof domes on a traditional bathhouse

A few yards along, just off the main street is the **House Museum of Vagif Mustafazadeh** (4 Vagif Mustafazadeh Lane; daily 10am–6pm), the home of the renowned composer (1940–1975) credited with combining traditional mugham with jazz to birth a new musical niche. Despite a ban during Soviet rule, Baku witnessed a boom in jazz music in the '60s and '70s, and hosts the annual Baku Jazz Festival (see page 92) every October. Vagif's house faces the 11th-century Muhammad Mosque, which got its name, Siniggala, meaning 'broken tower', when its minaret was damaged (later restored) by the Russian Army during the Russo-Persian war of 1722–1723.

Also on this street is the 18th-century **Aga Mikayil Bath House ❻** (daily 11am–10pm; Mon and Fri women only), the city's oldest and most spacious hammam. It's protected by the state as an 'architectural monument of national value'; it is square with curved arches and an oddly-shaped chimney. This particular area used to be called 'hamamçilar mahalası', meaning bathkeepers area, and although the culture of bath-houses isn't as popular as it used to be, you'll still find some locals who swear by their healing and nurturing properties. **Taze Bey Hamami** (tel: 12-492 6440; www.tazebey.az; daily 9am–1am) a couple of streets away on Sheikh Shamil Street is also a favourite with locals and tourists.

When it comes to art, the last decade has been a game changer for Baku, and even though most of the larger museums and galleries are outside of the Old City, Kichik Gala and its vicinity offers some unexpected art galleries, like the contemporary **YAY Gallery** (Tue–Sun noon–8pm) and, on Ilyas Efendiyev Street, **Tahir Salahov House Museum** (Tue–Sun 9am–6pm), which celebrates the works of Azerbaijan's greatest living painter, who uses his art to depict the harsh conditions of life under Soviet rule. Also here is **Absheron Art Gallery** (Mon–Sat 10am–6pm) on Asef Zeynalli Street, right next to the Absheron Sharab wine store.

Nearby is the 12th-century **Juma Mosque**, said to be built on the site of a Zoroastrian temple, as well as the stone-faced **Museum of Archaeology and Ethnography**. Next to the area's Shamakhi Gate, on Boyuk Gala Street you'll find **Baku Khan's**

⦿ HAMMAM RITUALS

Hammams have been integral to Azerbaijan's culture for centuries. More so in the Middle Ages, when every neighbourhood (known as mahalla) in Baku had its own hammam and mosque, and it was customary for Bakuvians to visit their local hammam once a week. They were places not only to relax and rejuvenate, but to get together to discuss important issues and matchmake for their sons and daughters. **Gasim Bey Bath**, near the Salyan gate of the Old City walls, is a historical monument and one of the city's most traditionally-designed hammams. Nicknamed 'Sweet', thanks to the sweets it served with tea, it was reconstructed in 1970 and now serves as a pharmacy. Opposite the Maiden Tower is another hammam treasure, the 15th-century **Haji Bani Bath Complex**.

Palace, the 18th- to 19th-century ruins of where the city's Khans used to live. It was used as a garrison when the Russian Empire occupied Baku in 1806. Plans to restore the buildings were announced in 2018.

PHILHARMONIA GARDEN

Located just outside the east wall of the Old City, this is Baku's oldest and arguably most beautiful park. Origins of the park itself date back to the 1830s, when it was just a small area with fruit trees. It became a fully-developed park by the end of the century. For years the locals called it Governor's Park, and it's where you'll find **Azerbaijan State Philharmonic Hall** ❼ (daily 11am–7pm), built in 1910–12 and originally used for public meetings. The venue is named after the famous Azerbaijani singer Muslim Magomayev (1942–2008), nick-named the 'Soviet Sinatra'. After the Soviets came into power in the 1920s, music fans in Baku would assemble inside this yellow Italian Renaissance-inspired building, which took archi-tectural inspiration from the casinos of Monte Carlo. Tickets for performances here are available at ticket offices or www.iticket.az, as are most theatre and concert tickets in Baku (see page 91).

Just behind Icheri Sheher metro station, in front of YAY Gallery, is the 10ft bronze bust of **Aliaga Vahid** (1895–1965), the country's renowned satirical poet. Take a closer look at his hair to spot carvings of allegorical characters depicting scenes of day-to-day life, from weddings and funerals to musicians and markets. Just behind the park is the **Azerbaijan Museum of National Art** ❽ (www.nationalartmuseum.az; Tue–Sun 10am–6pm), which consists of two buildings housing over 3,000 pieces of art and sculptures by artists from Azerbaijan, Russia, Iran, Turkey and across Europe.

BOULEVARD AND NEFTCHILAR AVENUE

The leafy, Caspian-front Baku Boulevard (Dənizkənarı Bulvar), or just 'Bulvar' to locals, has been the stamping ground of Azeris since 1909, and it's where you will find them aimlessly strolling, gossiping and sipping black tea until late. Today, it seems worlds away from the oil derrick days of the 20th century, a time when the oil boom was in full swing and the coast was dotted with mansions of oil barons. Back then, the smell of oil in the streets was unavoidable, and many of its sections, unlike now, were not open to the public.

In 2009, in celebration of its centennial anniversary, the promenade underwent a colossal extension and makeover, and now stretches 25km (16 miles) along the coast in its entirety, with everything from teahouses and restaurants to a Ferris wheel and a multi-storey shopping centre situated in between.

More traditionally, and for most of its existence, it ran from National Flag Square in the west to Freedom Square in the east. This is a particularly popular area during the summer, when the cool breeze from the sea eases Baku's torrid temperatures. Live like an Azeri and spend a leisurely evening here, and take in the fountains, the carefully-planted gardens and the buzz of the cafés and fairgrounds that have opened up here.

Neftchilar Avenue (Neftçilər Prospekti), named after the oil workers of Baku, is one of the city's main roads and runs parallel to the Bulvar, starting at Azneft Square and stretching all the way to Port Baku Park. The street is dotted with international designer labels, hotels and some of Baku's most iconic architecture, like the grandiose Government House. It is also a large stretch of the Baku City Circuit for the Formula 1 Azerbaijan Grand Prix every April. A leisurely stroll is an unbeatable way of exploring this area, but if you are in a hurry, buses 5, 6 and 88 run up and down regularly.

FREEDOM SQUARE

At the east end of Neftchilar Avenue is **Freedom Square** (also Azadliq Square), the largest square in the centre of Baku. Previously named after Soviet Union leader

Freedom Square

Vladimir Lenin, it changed its name after Azerbaijan gained independence in 1991. It is home to **Government House 9**, a mammoth, Baroque building and one of Baku's most iconic constructions from the Soviet era. Also known as Dom Soviet, the impressive edifice was built between 1938 and 1952 by architects Lev Rudnev, V.O. Munts and K. Tkachenko, and now houses several of the country's state ministries. The towering, bronze statue of Lenin that once stood in the front of the building was removed in 1990 during Azerbaijan's bloody fight for freedom.

> ### Very superstitious
>
> Wherever you go in the country, you're never too far from superstitious beliefs, and most of them are related to marriage. Things that are believed to bring bad luck include cutting your nails at night, sweeping in the afternoon or touching someone's feet with a straw broom known as a *süpürgə*.

Today, this is where the celebrations for the Day of the Armed Forces of Azerbaijan take place, as well as a number of other parades. See if you can catch a performance of the Seven Beauties, a colourful musical fountain where the water dances to music by Azerbaijani and international composers. Across the road is Park Bulvar Mall, a multi-storey shopping centre which opened in 2010.

THE MUSEUM CENTER

A short walk west on Neftchilar Avenue is the pillar-fronted **Museum Center 10** (www.museumcenter.az; Tue–Sun 10am–6pm). The four-storey complex, which sits across the road from a large fountain display and the now-defunct Parachute Tower, was formerly a branch of the Moscow Lenin Museum, and

Crossing the road

Beware that it's against Azerbaijani law to cross the street if there's an underpass available. There are several underpasses on Neftchilar Avenue, and some with escalators, to make crossing this busy, six-lane road easier.

now houses three separate museums; Azerbaijan State Museum of Musical Culture, home to thousands of traditional musical instruments including tar, kamancha and ney; the Museum of Independence of Azerbaijan and the Azerbaijan State Theater Museum.

A little further down on Haji Zeynalabdin Taghiyev Street is the largest museum in all of Azerbaijan, the **National Museum of History of Azerbaijan** ⓫ (tel: 12-4932 387; www.azhistorymuseum.az; Tue–Sun 10am–6pm). The Italian Renaissance-style mansion, built by Polish architect Jozef Goslawski, was the former home of industrial magnate Haji Zeynalabdin Taghiyev, and now exhibits over 300,000 items, immortalising Azerbaijan's history from the Stone Age to the 20th century. On the next street is the **House-Museum of Samad Vurgun** (4 Tarlan Aliyarbekov Street; Tue–Sun 10am–6pm), the country's celebrated poet, scientist and public figure, Samad Vurgun (1906–1956), laureate of two USSR State Prizes.

BAKU PUPPET THEATRE

Further west of the avenue will take you to the pastel-yellow, neoclassical **Baku Puppet Theatre** ⓬ (Abdulla Şaiq adına Azərbaycan Dövlət Kukla Teatrı; tel: 12-492 6425; performances Tue–Sun July–Sept), built by Polish architect **Jozef Plosko** (1867–1931) in 1910. It was initially the 'Phenomenon' cinema, and over the years has also served as a casino, the

Satyragite Theatre and an agriculture museum, finally becoming the puppet theatre in 1931.

The folk art of puppetry in Azerbaijan is said to go back to the Middle Ages, and the sizes of the dolls here range from just a few centimetres to double human size. Performances are mostly fairy tales and local folk stories, and most of them are in Azerbaijani, but occasionally Russian and Turkish.

As well as the Baku Puppet Theatre, Jozef Ploszko was the man behind a number of other architectural gems in Baku. In the late 19th century, he was invited to the city by fellow Pole Jozef Goslawski, the architect who built the Baroque **Baku City Executive Power** in between Kichik Gala and Istiglaliyyat Street. Ploszko soon became the architect of Musa Naghiyev, one of the city's wealthiest oil magnates. In 1907, when

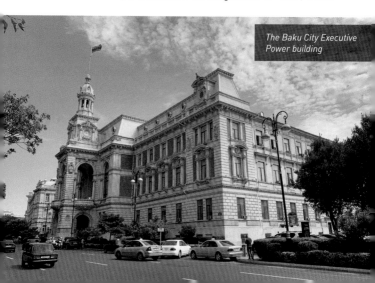

The Baku City Executive Power building

Naghiyev purchased the Nikolayevskaya area (now Istiglaliyyat Street), he asked Ploszko to build him a mansion in honour of his late son, and so was born the Gothic-style **Ismailiyya Palace** ⓭. It was inspired by Doge's Palace in Venice and later became the **Academy of Sciences.**

Ploszko's other notable designs include the neo-Gothic **Palace of Happiness** (6 Murtuza Mukhtarov) in the Narimanov district, now the Palace of Marriage Registrations, and the

⦿ HAJI ZEYNALABDIN TAGHIYEV

One of the Russian Empire's most notable rags-to-riches story is that of Azerbaijani philanthropist and oil baron Haji Zeynalabdin Taghiyev (1838–1924). After being born into a poor family in the Old City, Taghiyev worked as a bricklayer until he was 35, when he hit the jackpot after discovering oil in a plot of land he'd purchased in the Bibi-Heybat area of Baku.

He used his fortune for philanthropy projects all across the city. As a passionate advocate of women's education, a revolutionary idea at the time, he went on to fund the very first Muslim girls boarding school (also called the Empress Alexandra Muslim School for Girls) in the Caucasus region, although it initially met with many challenges. The school, designed by Jozef Goslawski, opened in 1900 and functioned until the collapse of the Russian Empire in 1918. Today, it serves as the **Institute of Manuscripts**, part of the Academy of Sciences on Istiglaliyyat Street just outside the Old City.

Taghiyev also funded the first textile factory in Baku, several fisheries and the Azerbaijan State Academic Opera and Ballet Theatre on Nizami Street. He is called the 'Father of the Nation' for all he has done for Baku.

original Church of the Blessed Virgin Mary's Immaculate Conception, built for the Polish community in Baku. The latter was demolished during the Soviet Union's anti-religious campaign in the 1930s.

AZNEFT SQUARE

At the very top of Neftchilar Avenue is **Azneft Square** ⑭, the buzzy heart of this area, where the tooting of car horns around the busy roundabout can be heard through the night. Here, at one of the main entrances to the Bulvar, you'll find a towering flag of Azerbaijan and a giant chessboard on the ground.

Directly ahead at the end of the pier is the Yacht Club, a hotel and restaurant complex built on stilts in the Caspian Sea. On the other side of the square is the Four Seasons Hotel Baku (see page 138), one of Baku's most picturesque hotels, and the **Palace of Seyid Mirbabayev**, the French Renaissance-style home of another oil tycoon, now the HQ of national oil and gas company SOCAR. From here, you'll see the peaks of the all-consuming **Flame Towers** (see page 62) poking the sky just over a mile away.

Up ahead on the boulevard is **Little Venice** ⓯, a mini town of two islands connected by bridges, where you can take a gondola ride for just a few manats.

AZERBAIJAN CARPET MUSEUM

Roughly 10,000 carpets, national garments and traditional ceramics are housed in the extravagant, rolled-carpet-shaped **Azerbaijan Carpet Museum** ⓰ (www.azcarpetmuseum.az; Tue–Fri 10am–6pm, Sat–Sun 10am–8pm), located right in the middle of the Bulvar. The seafront, three-storey museum was designed by Austrian architect Franz Janza,

---

⊘ BAKUCARD

The handy BakuCard covers public transport across the city, plus discounts for the airport shuttle, half price on the hop-on, hop-off Baku City Tour, free or discounted entry to a selection of museums and attractions, and special offers at shops and restaurants. Cards are available online (www.bakucard.az) and at the airport, major hotels, tourism agencies and www.iticket.az kiosks.

Tickets cost 24 AZN, 45 AZN or 70 AZN for one, three or seven days. Over 300 partners include cultural attractions like Azerbaijan Carpet Museum, Shirvanshah's Palace and the Ateshgah & Yanar Dag Group Tour, as well as popular bars and restaurants like Mugam Klub, Sumakh and ROOM (see page 110).

and houses carpets dating from between the 17th and 21st centuries, from various regions across the country. Founded in 1967 by artist and carpet weaver Latif Karimov (1906–1991), the museum relocated a couple of times before opening here in 2014, and also serves as a research centre for the ancient art of carpet-weaving, something that has been an important part of Azerbaijani culture since the Bronze Age.

International Mugham Center of Azerbaijan

Traditionally, carpets in Azerbaijan are divided into four categories according to design and technique; Guba-Shirvan, Ganja-Gazakh, Karabakh and Tabriz. They are mostly made from lamb or sheep's wool. Sheki in northeastern Azerbaijan is the only region in the country to produce silk, making the cost of a silk carpet much higher. Carpets are sold in the museum's shop and in many shops in the Old City. The website has details of current exhibitions showing the work of local artists and weavers. Be aware that you cannot take anything antique (pre-1960) out of the country, including carpets. For anything dated 1960 or after, you still require an export certificate, which you can obtain at the museum (see page 89 for details).

A few yards from the museum is the **International Mugham Center of Azerbaijan** (Mon–Fri 9am–6pm), home to festivals and concerts dedicated to preserving mugham (*muğam*), an

The Baku Eye

ancient, melancholic musical genre integral to Azerbaijan's DNA. The design of the building incorporates elements of the tar, a traditional long-necked string instrument key to mugham. The other main instrument used in a mugham performance is the stringed kamancha.

Just a little further down, projecting out to sea, is the striking **Caspian Waterfront Mall**, a five-storey, 120,000 sq metres (1.2 million sq ft) entertainment complex that's still under construction. Designed by London-based architects Chapman Taylor, the eight-sided building is quite clearly inspired by the geometric shapes of the Sydney Opera House, with a glass flame protruding through its centre, a nod to Azerbaijan's appellation, the 'land of fire'.

Along this route, and also built out over the sea, is **Baku Eye** ⓱ (daily 1pm–1am), the boulevard's Ferris wheel, which is a pleasant way of spending 15 minutes for panoramic views of the bay and city. Unlike the one in London, there's hardly ever a queue here, and it's best to ride this at night when Baku Bay becomes a sea of lights. Just be aware that it does not operate during extreme weather conditions. Towards the west end of the boulevard, things quieten down a little bit until you reach the National Flag Square (see page 50).

SABAYIL CASTLE

The Sabail district shares its name with a submerged castle that's shrouded in mystery. **Sabayil Castle** ⓲, nicknamed the Atlantis of the Caspian Sea, was built on a small island in the 13th century, and sits underwater just in front of the Baku Eye. Researchers have suggested that the fortress, which was 180 metres/yds long and 40 metres/yds wide, was either used as a defence system or a caravanserai, and it became submerged during a powerful earthquake in 1306. Due to fluctuating water levels, the top of the castle's ruins have become visible at times. There are underground tunnels that connect the castle to the Old City, and some of its relics can be found in the courtyard of Shirvanshah's Palace. It is not certain why, how or who built this misfortuned fortress, or the tunnels running beneath it.

Sabayil Castle ruins exposed

Baku Crystal Hall concert arena

NATIONAL FLAG SQUARE

The considerable height of the flag at **National Flag Square** ⓲ (Bayraq meydanı), in the settlement of Bayil, was once recognised by the Guinness World Records as the tallest in the world, but has since been overtaken by the 165m/yd pole in Dushanbe, Tajikistan. For any vexillophiles, the base of the pole, built in the shape of an eight-pointed star, also serves as the National Flag Museum, housing flags, medals and other ceremonial items from Azerbaijan.

The square is adjacent to **Baku Crystal Hall** (www.crystalhall. az), the glittering, purpose-built concert arena that hosted the 57th Eurovision Song Contest in 2012. In between the National Flag Square and Aquatics Palace (host venue of the Baku 2015 European Games) is **YARAT Contemporary Art Space** ⓳ (www. yarat.az; Tue–Sun 11am–8pm). Founded in 2011 by local artist Aida Mahmudova, the not-for-profit centre for local and international contemporary art is housed inside of a converted 1960s naval base. YARAT, which means 'create' in Azerbaijani, is home to quirky exhibitions, workshops and art festivals, and the helpful guides here are more than happy to show you around and talk about what's on show. There's also a Mexican restaurant here.

DOWNTOWN AND FOUNTAINS SQUARE

On the northeastern tip of the Sabail district, just a short walk from the boulevard and Old City, is Baku's commercial

⊙ EUROVISION IN BAKU

Azerbaijan started entering the Eurovision Song Contest in 2008. When duo Ell & Nikki (Eldar Gasimov and Nigar Jamal) scored the country's first ever win just three years later in 2011 with their song 'Running Scared', it sparked celebrations all over the streets of Baku. Consequently, the boulevard was then extended west to the National Flag Square, in time to host the contest at the purpose-built Baku Crystal Hall in 2012.

'Winning Eurovision back in 2011 gave me indescribable feelings', said Eldar Gasimov. 'I was very proud to be part of something so huge that put my country on the map. I think hosting Eurovision in Baku gave us a wonderful opportunity to show the world why people should visit Azerbaijan. We became part of a huge musical community', he added. To this day, the Azeri capital is the furthest east that the Eurovision Song Contest has ever been held, as well as the most expensive. It was here that Loreen, the Swedish contestant, won by a landslide with her hit 'Euphoria', which is often voted the best Eurovision winner of all time.

neighbourhood. Here you will find the chandelier-lined **Nizami Street**, one of Baku's main streets fringed with a wealth of shops, businesses and local restaurants (see page 55), as well international names like Hard Rock Cafe. The grand street, named after Azerbaijan's famed poet Nizami Ganjavi, is mostly pedestrianised and stretches 3.5km (2.2 miles) through the centre of the city; locals often refer to it by its Soviet-era name Torgovaya, Russian for 'Merchant Street'. The architectural style of the street has been likened to the opulence of Paris' avenues.

FOUNTAINS SQUARE

Adjacent to Nizami Street is **Fountains Square ㉑** (Fəvvarələr Meydanı), the favourite haunt of Azeris and the go-to place if you are unsure of what to do with your evening in Baku. You will find everything you need in this neighbourhood, from the expected restaurants and shops to theatres, museums, supermarkets, banks, apartments, cinemas and plenty of parks and benches.

This verdant, vibrant square, also called by its Soviet-era name Parapet, is a popular stamping ground of Azerbaijanis old and young, particularly after business hours and at weekends. The square's history goes back to the early 19th century when it started life as a wasteland. It was given the name Parapet, a French or Italian word for a low wall, most likely because of the fence that once bordered the square.

Having undergone a significant makeover in 2010, it's now an immaculate hang-out space encompassed by a little bit of everything: popular Azerbaijani restaurants like Firuze and Nargiz (see page 112), pubs, boutiques, a carousel and plenty of places to sit and while away the day. Occasionally, the square also hosts public festivals and celebrations like the one

Fountains Square is a popular nighttime haunt

in March to commemorate Novruz, the Azerbaijani New Year, one of the country's biggest national holidays.

Its modern name, Fountains Square, comes from the dozens of fountain installations first built here during the Soviet era, each one with its individual style, some traditional, and some that are giant reflective spheres, popular for taking fisheye style photos. It's also home to, quite bizarrely, the world's largest KFC restaurant, housed in the former Sabunchi railway station, which was part of the first electric railway system in the USSR.

In the 1960s and 70s, this area was the location of several Soviet films like the cult classic Amphibian Man. Look out for quirky details around the square, like the bronze statue of a girl sitting on a bench and typing on her phone, and the tiny little hippos with their mouths ajar around one of the fountains.

Close by is **Molokan Gardens** (Khagani Park), one of Baku's oldest parks, with a playground, fountains and a restaurant with live music. Just by here is an eye-catchingly colourful florist.

NATIONAL MUSEUM OF AZERBAIJAN LITERATURE

In between Fountains Square and the Old City Walls is **Nizami Park**, dedicated to Azerbaijani poet Nizami Ganjavi and home to the statue-graced **National Museum of Azerbaijan Literature** ㉒ (www.nizamimuseum.az; daily 11am–5pm).

The museum was established in 1939 to commemorate the country's most famed poets and authors, and first opened its doors to the public in 1945. Its facade is painfully photogenic with blue, majolica ogives bearing the statues of six literary greats; Fizuli, Vagif, M.F.Akhundov, Natavan,

⊙ POET NIZAMI GANJAVI

The 12th-century poet and thinker Nizami Ganjavi (1141–1209) was born and died in Ganja, Azerbaijan's second largest city in the west of the country, around 300km (186 miles) west of Baku. As well as literature, he is praised for his knowledge of medicine, theology, philosophy, music, arts and astronomy. The poet wrote in the Persian language, as was literary custom at the time, and is buried in a mausoleum in Ganja.

Among Nizami's most popular poems is **Leyli and Majnun**, bearing a similar plot to Romeo and Juliet, although it predates Shakespeare by over 1,000 years. The poem was turned into an opera in 1908, with music composed by Uzeyir Hajibeyli, and is considered to be the first opera in the Muslim world.

J.Mammadguluzade and J.Jabbarli, and there is an equally photogenic entrance door on the side of the building. The museum, with 23 exhibition halls, is home to over 3,000 rare books, portraits, sculptures and memoirs, and guided tours are available in English.

In Nizami Park you will find a statue of celebrated poet **Nizami Ganjavi** (you will see his name a lot in Baku) atop a set of stairs. Like most places in Baku, the museum and park are best admired at dusk when everything is dimly lit.

NIZAMI STREET AREA

In the middle of Nizami Street is the **Azerbaijan State Academic Opera and Ballet Theater** ㉓ (Opera Və Balet Teatrı; Nizami Street; tel: 12-493 3188), a neo-Gothic opera house built in 1910–11 by architect Nikolai Bayev, who entwined Baroque, Rococo and Moorish architectural styles.

The reason behind the existence of the opera house is somewhat unusual. In 1910, when Russian soprano Antonina Nezhdanova visited Baku to perform at various venues, one of the Mailov brothers (a trio of oil magnates) fell in love with the glamorous singer and began showering her with jewellery. When Nezhdanova was asked to return to Baku, she refused to do so, expressing her disappointment at the lack of an opera house in such a wealthy city. That's when Mailov promised her that if she returns in a year, he will have an opera house waiting for her. True to his word, Mailov had the 1800-seated opera house built in just 10 months, and Nezhdanova returned to celebrate its opening. It was renovated in 1987 and today produces an array of shows from classical plays and operas to dance groups and ballet performances. Check www.iticket.az to see what is on during your visit.

Sahil Bagı (Coastal Garden) is a peaceful garden a short walk away on Uzeyir Hajibeyov Street, lined with benches and a golden fountain, perfect for a few moments of peace away from the main street.

Adjacent to the park, overlooking Khagani Street, Nizami Street and Rashid Behbudov Street is the grand **National Library of Azerbaijan** (www.anl.az; Tue–Sun 10am–8pm), another example of the city's beautiful statue-encrusted buildings. It was founded in 1922. The library, which consists of 24 departments, is reported to house around 4.5 million items and has a reading room which holds around 500 people.

On the corner of Nizami Street and Rashid Behbudov Street is the **Rashid Behbudov State Song Theatre** (tel: 12-493 9415; daily) named after the celebrated singer and actor. The theatre, which used to be a synagogue in the early 1900s, is built in the Greek Revival style, and its repertoire focusses on musical styles like folk, mugham and tasnif.

National Library of Azerbaijan

Just off the main road on Samad Vurgun Street is the statue of yet another celebrated poet, **Imadeddin Nasimi** (1369–1417).

NASIMI AND YASAMAL

The two central districts of Nasimi and Yasamal, both situated slightly north of Sabail and the boulevard, don't have much in the way of typical tourist attractions, but offer plenty of spacious parks if you have a spare afternoon and fancy strolling somewhere away from the bustle of the city centre. In Baku, as a general rule, the further you go from the Caspian bay, the less there is to see and the more residential the neighbourhoods become.

Nasimi (named after acclaimed poet Imadaddin Nasimi), a few blocks north of the boulevard, is home to the city's main transport hub, Baku Central Railway Station, which links the city to destinations around the country as well as running daily trains to Tbilisi, the capital of neighbouring Georgia. The 28 May Metro Station, named after the country's Independence Day, runs all three of Baku's metro lines. which will take you to almost anywhere in the city. A short walk from here is Taza Bazar (see page 87), the largest market in all of Baku, and also Baku State Circus. The rectangular-shaped Winter Park, sometimes called Fuzuli Park (after another one of Azerbaijan's poetry greats), runs for 600 metres/yds on the southern edge of the district.

Bordering Yasamal (which means 'flat area on top of mountain or hill' in Azerbaijani) is mostly known for education institutes, Teze Pir Mosque and the now-demolished historic neighbourhood of Sovetski, which has been transformed into

Quiet street in Yasamal

Central Park. North of here is the Binagadi raion, home to the 2012-built Heydar Mosque, the largest in the Caucasus.

FUZULI STREET

Straddling the southern border of Nasimi and Yasamal districts is the 2km (1.2-mile) -long Fuzuli Street, flanked with green parks, music venues and 28 Mall, a multistory shopping centre with a cinema. On the east end of the street, at the centre of four busy roads, is the lush **Heydar Aliyev Park**, named after the third president of Azerbaijan, where you can walk among fountains, trees and colourful flower beds.

> ### The great Nasimi
>
> In 2019, the International Astronomical Union named a minor planet after the celebrated poet and thinker, Imadaddin Nasimi, to mark the 650th anniversary of his birth. Nasimi is known for penning some 300 poems in Arabic, Persian and Azerbaijani.
>
> In September 2018, Baku hosted the first Nasimi Festival of Poetry, Arts and Spirituality, celebrating the poet's work in both Baku and Shamakhi, his native city.

Here you will find the **Heydar Aliyev Palace** (formerly known as Lenin Palace), one of the city's key music venues, which hosts a series of concerts and was also the venue for President Ilham Aliyev's inauguration in 2008.

Further along the street is **Winter Park** ㉔ (also known as Fuzuli Park), wedged in between Fuzuli Street and Shamshi Badalbeyli Street, home to ubiquitous sandstone buildings and plenty of seating areas with free Wi-Fi amid olive trees and city views. There are also a handful of restaurants and cafés here, and, on one end, the pillar-fronted **Azerbaijan State Academic Drama Theater**, the foundations of which

Azerbaijan State
Academic Drama Theater

were first laid in 1873. It has a repertoire that ranges from the works of William Shakespeare to local comedies and dramas.

CENTRAL PARK (FORMERLY SOVETSKI)

Continue a few yards west on Fuzuli Street and into Yasamal district to explore the verdant **Central Park ㉕** (Mərkəzi Park), an extension of Fuzuli Park, which runs vertically from north to south.

This area was formerly known as Sovetski, a historic residential neighbourhood that was built during the first oil boom of Baku, and was once home to hundreds of residents, historic mosques, low-rise houses and bath houses. In 2013, work began to demolish the area, and eventually the new park, designed by Austrian architect Jens Hoffmann, was opened in the spring of 2019. Spend an hour or so here meandering the new pathways along with the seven playgrounds, two cafés and nine fountains.

At one end of the park, on top of a hill, is the majestic **Teze Pir Mosque** ㉖, completed in 1914 and designed by Ziver bey Ahmadbeyov, the Chief Architect of Baku from 1918–1925 and the first Azeri architect ever to receive a European vocational degree. The functioning mosque, financed by female philanthropist Nabat Khanum Ashurbeyova, boasts a three-arched portico, twin minarets and a marble dome with decorative touches all in gold. Be aware that to enter the mosque, men and women must enter through separate doors.

A short walk west to Landau Street will take you to another one of Yasamal's leisurely parks, **Huseyn Cavid Park** (named after yet another of Azerbaijan's famed poets), where you can cycle, enjoy the ample shaded seating or duck into one of the cafés for a refreshing tea.

Just across Huseyn Javid Avenue is the picture-perfect **Akademia Garden**, home to the Azerbaijan National Academy of Sciences (www.science.gov.az) built by architect Mikayil Huseynov, the man behind the Nizami Cinema Center and the Baku Academy of Music. Friends of Jazz, formerly Baku Jazz Club, (tel: 12-538 2868; www.jazz.az) is also close by on Nariman Narimanov Avenue and aims to revive Baku's jazz culture with festivals, competitions and gigs.

THE FLAME TOWERS AND WEST OF THE CITY CENTRE

Long before the Flame Towers were erected, this area, roughly 2km (1.2 miles) southeast of the Old City, was known mostly for Alley of Martyrs, a war memorial park and cemetery. Up until the dissolution of the Soviet Union, this area was called Kirov Park (now Highland Park), thanks to the gargantuan statue of Bolshevik leader Sergei Kirov that once towered over the city. His statue, much like almost all Soviet leader monuments, was dismantled shortly after the collapse of the Soviet Union.

If you head further west from here, chances are you are en route to Gobustan National Park, but there are a handful of undiscovered gems along the way, like the Naftalan Health Center (see page 64) where you can try one of Azerbaijan's oldest, and most peculiar, health rituals, or the Central Botanical Garden, which is perfect for peace and quiet and an abundance of nature.

THE FLAME TOWERS

A five-minute car journey (or a 30 minute walk uphill) from Azneft Square will take you to the **Flame Towers** ㉗, a trio of mammoth, flame-shaped towers that are a nod to Azerbaijan's nickname, the 'land of fire'. Designed by US-based firm HOK and completed in 2012, they can be seen from almost all points in the city centre, and have totally transformed the city's sky-line and become a symbol of modern Baku.

Come night-time, 10,000 animated LED screens light up these towers in the colours of flames and the Azeri flag. The tallest tower (182 metres/597ft) is used for residential apart-ments, the second (165 metres/541ft) houses the five-star Fairmont Baku Hotel and the third tower (131 metres/430ft) serves as office space. Unless you're staying at the hotel or meeting someone there for drinks, there's very little point in getting close to the towers as they are best admired in all their glittering glory from a distance.

A 15-minute walk via Mehdi Huseyn Street will take you to the **Green Theatre** (Yaşıl Teatr; tel: 12-492 2637), an amphitheatre of 2,500 green chairs built in the 60s under the orders of the then mayor, Alish Lemberansky. If you fancy visiting, it is best to call in advance to see which concerts are currently running.

ALLEY OF MARTYRS

Take the recently-renovated funicular (the full journey takes 7–10 minutes) from Shovkat Alakbarova Street just off Neftchilar Avenue to the **Alley of Martyrs** ㉘ (Şəhidlər Xiyabanı; open all hours) on Mehdi Huseyn Street. This is one of Baku's most sombre attractions. The cemetery and memorial park is dedicated to those who were killed on 20 January 1990, also known as Black January, the day that the Soviet Army murdered civilians in Baku in an attempt to suppress Azerbaijan's movement for independence. The memorial is also the resting place of those who were killed in the Nagorno-Karabakh War (see page 22) as well as the Battle of Baku (1918).

At the top of the lane is the Eternal Flame Monument with a large burning flame at its centre – don't get too close, the flame is strong and very hot. Just next to it is **Highland Park**, a garden and park located on the highest point in all of Baku, where you will find spectacular views of the city, especially at dusk. You

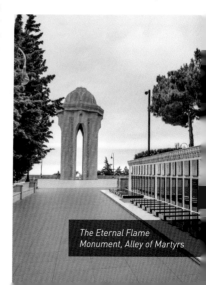

The Eternal Flame Monument, Alley of Martyrs

Photography

It's OK to take photos in most places, except for a handful of state facilities where you need to seek permission first. When capturing locals, especially in the Old City or less-explored areas, again, it's always better to ask permission before you snap.

can also enjoy a drink at the Dagustu Park Café (daily 11am–midnight).

The twin-minaret Mosque of the Martyrs here, also known as the Turkish Mosque, was built in the early 1990s. Further up on Parliament Avenue is the **Alley of Honor** (Fəxri Xiyaban), a cemetery and the resting place of many notable figures, including the much-respected former president Heydar Aliyev.

If you are a nature lover, walk a few minutes northwest to **Central Botanical Garden** ㉙ (Mikayil Mushfiq; www.bakubo-tanicalgarden.az; daily, summer 9am–8pm, winter 8am–6pm), a lush garden founded in 1934. It is home to an estimated 2,000 species of local and exotic trees and plants, as well as 125 rare endangered species. The garden is a hotspot for locals and tourists seeking peace and shade in the summer months, but is also an oasis for scientists carrying out research for plant resources across Azerbaijan. There is also a small café serving tea and snacks. It's worth noting that although there is an entry charge, it's just 1 AZN (50p).

NAFTALAN HEALTH CENTER

One of Azerbaijan's most peculiar traditions involves bathing in a tub full of thick, warm crude oil. Just 3.5km (2.2 miles) west of the Alley of Martyrs is **Naftalan Health Center** (Naftalan Sağlamlıq Mərkəzi Bakı; 1 Mikayil Mushfig Street; tel: 12-448 3766; www.naftalan-booking.com), where guests can submerge themselves in a rare type of oil called Naftalan, also the name of the city in western Azerbaijan where the oil originates. Why? The oil, nicknamed 'black gold', is said to have numerous healing properties, from relieving chronic arthritis to curing eczema and psoriasis. However, not everyone agrees with its suggested medicinal powers.

The most famous resort for this unrefined treatment is in the city of Naftalan itself, but if you are in Baku and are intrigued (and brave), the Naftalan Health Centre recommends starting with dipping in the oil for 10 minutes, after which you are wiped down and required to take several showers to wash everything off. Treatments start from 24–30 AZN, and the number of treatments required is prescribed to you by the on-site doctor.

Submerged in a crude oil bath at the Naftalan Health Center

The processing of this unique oil took off during the oil boom in the 19th century, although it's suggested that people started bathing in the gooey substance as early as the 6th century. Both poet Nizami Ganjavi and explorer Marco Polo have mentioned Naftalan oil in their works. A legend surrounding the magical healing powers of the oil is that during medieval times, a herder left behind a sick donkey who rolled into a pool of oil in its dying state, and when the herder returned weeks later, the donkey had miraculously been cured.

BIBI-HEYBAT

A few kilometres southwest of central Baku is Bibi-Heybat, where the world's first oil well was dug in 1846, over a decade before the famous oil rush of Pennsylvania, United States, in 1859.

The main attraction here is the **Bibi-Heybat Mosque** ㉚ just off Salyan Highway, built in 1998 as a replica of the original,

---

⊘ THE OIL MAN

Georgian-born artist Sabir Chopuroghlu substitutes paint with Naftalan oil to create visually intriguing images using his nails and fingers alone. The golden and dark brown-hued images, which include scenes of Baku, wildlife and nature, are all exhibited in his studio as well as across hotels in both Naftalan and Baku.

The artist got his big break when his work was showcased in Germany, and he also created a special painting dedicated to the Eurovision Song Contest in 2012. Swing by **his studio** on 92 Mirmahmud Kazimovski Street (in the Binagadi district, slightly north of the border of Nasimi) to admire his work and purchase one of these truly unique creations for yourself.

which was destroyed as part of Joseph Stalin's mission to ban all religious practises across the Soviet Union. It's worth stopping here on your way to or from Gobustan National Park to admire the mosque's dominating twin minarets and impressive interior, decorated in emerald green and gold. A five-minute walk from here is the restaurant Nar & Sharab, which is a hit with locals and turns into a fun beach club during the summer months.

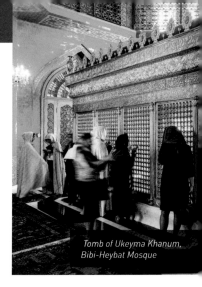

Tomb of Ukeyma Khanum, Bibi-Heybat Mosque

EAST OF THE CITY CENTRE

East of central Baku is comprised mainly of shopping centres, sporting venues and university grounds. Most of these are situated in the Narimanov raion, named after Bolshevik revolutionary Nariman Narimanov, whose statue (in Yasamal raion) is one of very few Soviet-era statues still standing in the city.

Over the last decade, the Narimanov district has witnessed a rather substantial makeover. In 2012, the striking, all-white Heydar Aliyev Center changed the face of the area and became one of modern Baku's most recognisable emblems, even making it onto stamps and the 200 AZN manat note. In 2015 the boulevard was extended to reach Baku White City in the southeast raion of Khatai. The area, once known as Baku Black

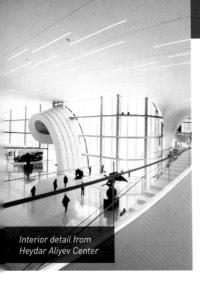

Interior detail from
Heydar Aliyev Center

City, was an industrial hub for the city's oil business, and is currently undergoing a significant urban regeneration.

The eastern part of the city also has a strong sporty reputation, and is home to several stadiums, like Baku Olympic Stadium.

BAKU MUSEUM OF MODERN ART

Just off the very east end of Neftchilar Avenue on Yusuph Safarov Street is the **Baku Museum of Modern Art** ㉛ (tel: 12-4908 404; www.moma.az; Tue–Sun 11am–8pm), also referred to as MIM, which houses an intriguing collection of work ranging from the mid-20th century to the present.

Most of the artwork here is by Azerbaijani artists, but there are also pieces from the private collections of avant-garde artists Picasso and Salvador Dali. The inside is all white, and a mishmash of paintings, sculptures and statues, with leather bean bags that make for the perfect viewing positions. The mastermind behind the museum's design is Bakuvian artist Altai Sadiqzadeh.

A short walk south from here will take you to New City Park just by the shipyard, filled with trees, fountains and benches. Think of it as Baku Boulevard's smaller, quieter little sister. Just to its left is Port Baku Park, another large seafront park with open spaces, a playground and benches to enjoy the cool sea breeze.

HEYDAR ALIYEV CENTER

The striking, meringue-like whirls of the **Heydar Aliyev Center** ③ (Heydər Əliyev Mərkəzi; www.heydaraliyevcenter. az; Tue–Fri 11am–7pm, Sat–Sun 11am–6pm) became part of Baku's cityscape in 2012. Designed by British-Iraqi architect Dame Zaha Hadid (1950-2016), the multi-functional complex is located slightly east of the city centre, around 6.7km (4.2 miles) from the Maiden Tower, and earned Hadid the Design of the Year award by London's Design Museum in 2014.

The abstract masterpiece regularly hosts concerts and interesting exhibitions, with collaborations including photojournalist Reza Deghati, singer Thomas Anders and painter and sculptor Zurab Tsereteli. It also features a three-storey museum on the history of Azerbaijan and the life and work of the former president Heydar Aliyev. Check online for what's on when you're visiting. Alternatively just go for a walk on the green surrounding the centre, where you're likely to spot locals relaxing and posing for pictures by the 'I Love Baku' sign.

The centre also hosts an annual retro car show with over 100 classic cars, all made before 1980, taking part in the exhibition and parading through the streets of Baku. The event is followed by a concert in the centre's park area.

Street names

The majority of the streets, as well as some parks and squares, are named after national heroes, including poets, scientists, singers and political figures. Note that a handful of streets are still called by their Soviet names, and although many of these were changed after the Soviet Union collapsed, some taxi drivers may still use them. If you're not sure, just get dropped off at the nearest landmark and walk.

TOFIQ BAHRAMOV REPUBLICAN STADIUM

The column-fronted **Tofiq Bahramov Republican Stadium** ③③
(Tofiq Bəhramov adına Respublika Stadionu; 10 Fatali Khan
Khoyski) in the Narimanov district opened in 1951 and is
the second largest stadium in Azerbaijan. This is where the
national football team used to play their games until they
moved further northeast to the Baku Olympic Stadium. Some
international games are still played here.

It's named after Tofiq Bahramov (1925–1993), the famous
Azerbaijani referee who awarded England the contentious
Geoff Hurst goal during the 1966 World Cup final against
West Germany, which went on to be England's first (and
only) triumph in the competition. In British press at the time,
although being born and raised in Azerbaijan, Bahramov was

Tofiq Bahramov Republican Stadium

mistakenly labelled as 'the Russian lineman' as Azerbaijan was part of the USSR at the time.

Further northeast in the Subunchi district is **Baku Olympic Stadium** ㉞, just by Boyukshor Lake, a 68,700-seat stadium that opened in 2015. It hosts national and international games and will be one of the venues for the UEFA Euro 2020 tournament. Aside from sport, the venue also hosts concerts.

Just next door is Ganjlik Mall, one of the largest shopping centres in the country, with a cinema, a bowling alley and a children's play area on the third floor. **Baku Zoological Park** (daily 10am–7pm), Azerbaijan's oldest zoo, founded in 1928, is also located here.

A short drive from here is another one of Baku's carpet institutions, **Azer Ilme Carpet Weaving Center** (Azər-İlmə Xalçaçılıq Mərkəzi; 2 Hamsi Rahimov Street; tel: 12-465 9036; www.azerilme.az; Mon–Sat 9am–6pm). Housed inside a grand building, here you can witness the entire carpet-making process, from how to dye yarn using natural means (in most cases these are colourful vegetables, like a red onion) and weave the thread to the washing, drying and ironing process. The centre employs weavers, teachers, restorers and dyers from all over the country. For carpet fanatics, there are silk and wool carpets to buy, and there is also a free tour, available in English.

Further east in Baku White City is **Luna Park**, where you will find an open-air cinema, fairground rides and places to eat and drink. Across the road is **Villa Petrolea** ㉟, first laid in 1882, and also the home of the **Nobel brothers**. The home is now a museum, the only one outside of the brothers' native Sweden. At the time, their company Branobel became the biggest oil company in the world, and it was the money Alfred Nobel earned from the company that ultimately led to the establishment of the coveted Nobel Prize (see page 21).

EXCURSIONS

Outside of the glittering cityscape of Baku, there is a wealth of history and things to do that warrant adding a couple more days onto your trip. With the rise of Baku's popularity in the last decade, there are now local English-speaking tour operators guiding tourists to the outlying attractions, when, once upon a time, the only way of seeing them was by taxi, and, if you were lucky, with a friend who spoke both English and Azerbaijani.

The petroglyph-filled Gobustan National Park, roughly 70km (43 miles) southwest of Baku, is one of the most unmissable historical excursions, and the area is also home to more than one third of the world's mud volcanoes. Travelling 25km (16 miles) east of the city will lead you to Ateshgah of Baku, an ancient Zoroastrian fire temple, and north is Yanar Dag, a mysterious mountainside that burns continuously through any weather. For anyone seeking a little relaxation, Baku also offers great beaches, particularly Bilgah, one of the cleanest and most popular in the city. And for nature enthusiasts, there are two additional national parks within an hour's drive from the centre of Baku.

For the most part, there is public transport that will take you to these places (just remember to tell the driver where you want to go), and they can easily be explored within a day. For tour details and bookings www.bakusightseeing.com is a good option for the main excursions. It offers fixed departure tours in English and Russian, and private tours in 11 languages.

GOBUSTAN

The Unesco-stamped **Gobustan National Park** 36 is an arid, mountainous stretch of land in Baku's Garadagh district that's

Mud volcano at Gobustan National Park

home to a freakish collection of primitive rock art and offers fantastic views of the Caspian Sea. If you're planning a day here, make sure to wear your walking/running shoes as the park grounds can be quite uneven (also beware of the scuttling lizards), and take a bottle of water, sunglasses and a hat, as there isn't much in the way here to shade you from the sweltering Baku sunshine.

The 6,000 or so etches in Gobustan, the oldest of which dates back 40,000 years, adorn the boulders and walls, and include dancing men, a headless pregnant woman, hunters, prayers, and a rampant goat. It's believed that they are attempts to chronicle human development here, and are a sign of the ceremonial and religious importance of this location between the Upper Palaeolithic period and the Middle Ages.

The small **Gobustan Museum** (www.gobustan-rockart.az; daily 10am–6pm) is definitely worth a visit, where you'll find artefacts like carving tools, unsettling taxidermy and helpful, digital illustrations of the extraordinary lives of those who lived here millennia ago. Norwegian explorer Thor Heyerdahl visited Azerbaijan regularly before his death in 2002, and grew fascinated with the rock carvings here. He believed that this area was the gateway for the mass migration of people to Scandinavia, a theory he formed after seeing the sickle-shaped boats drawn on the rocks that resembled those in his native Scandinavia. Information at the Gobustan Museum is provided in both Azerbaijani and English, and there is also a binocular viewing area.

The Gobustan region is also home to yet another of Baku's most unusual draws, the **mud volcanoes**. Azerbaijan is home to more mud volcanoes (roughly 350 out of 800) than any other

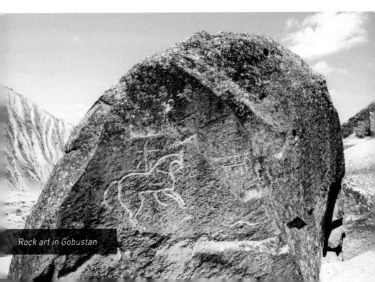

Rock art in Gobustan

country in the world, and these unusual, bubbling and occasionally explosive freaks of nature mainly consist of marsh gas, hydrocarbons and ineffective gasses. Some people believe that the mud has medicinal properties.

As a result of these volcanoes, there are eight islands in the archipelago of Baku. Eruptions are not common, but the most recent one was that of volcano

Ateshgah of Baku

Otman Bozdag in September 2018, which sent plumes up to 300m (980ft) high into the sky and caused cracks of 40 metres (130ft) deep.

Northeast from here, halfway between Baku and Gobustan, are the Khazar Islands, the ambitious yet stalled project to build a set of manmade islands that includes the tentative Azerbaijan Tower, which, if built, would become the tallest structure in the world at over a kilometre high.

ATESHGAH OF BAKU

Around 20km (12 miles) to the east of Baku is **Ateshgah of Baku** ❸ (daily 9am–6pm), a walled, religious site that once served as a holy place for the Zoroastrians, Hindus and Sikhs of Azerbaijan, and a must-see when you're in Baku. The site of Ateshgah, which means 'house of fire' in Persian, is believed to have been sacred since ancient times thanks to its naturally occurring, unquenchable fires, but the pentagonal temple that exists today in the courtyard was built between the late 16th century and the early 17th century. This is where a fire continuously burned naturally until 1969 – now pipe gas supplies the flame.

Zoroastrianism, a religion where fire is one of the sacred elements, first spread in Azerbaijan in the first millennium BCE, long before the construction of the temple. As the 7th century Arab conquest of Persia slowly started to eliminate Zoroastrianism, the predominant religion became Islam, and most Zoroastrians left for India where the largest community still exists today. However, the ancient religion still plays an integral role in Azerbaijani culture. For example, celebrations for Novruz, the coming of spring and the Persian New Year, involves jumping over a large bonfire, lighting a candle for every member of the family and baking the moon-shaped

⊘ LAND OF FIRE

There are a number of reasons why Azerbaijan has the moniker 'land of fire'. According to Persian sources, one of the first names for the country was 'Aturpatakan', meaning 'a place where sacred fire is preserved'. The South Caucasus region is said to be one of the first places where fire was used, and the fire-worshipping religion of Zoroastrianism was strong here until the arrival of Islam.

Today, Azerbaijan's relationship with fire burns on; at sites such as Yanar Dag and Ateshgah of Baku, through modern architecture like the Flame Towers, as well as the official symbol of the country, where a flame sits among the colours of the national flag.

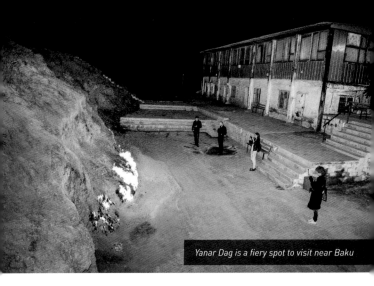
Yanar Dag is a fiery spot to visit near Baku

pastry şəkərbura, all a nod to the country's ever-present Zoroastrian past.

The low-rise cells dotted around the complex, where you will find inscriptions in Sanskrit, now serve as a museum where information about the area and the significance of Zoroastrianism is available in both Azerbaijani and English.

YANAR DAG

Combine your visit to Ateshgah of Baku with the nearby **Yanar Dag** ③⑧ (www.yanardag.az; May–Oct Sun–Thu 10am–8pm, Fri–Sat 10am–9pm, Nov–Apr Sun–Thu 10am–6pm, Fri–Sat 10am–7pm), another one of the country's fiery attractions. Meaning 'burning mountain' in Azerbaijani, Yanar Dag is a 10-metres (33ft) -wide hillside fire that's said to have been burning continuously for over 20,000 years. It is located in an arid expanse around 27km (17 miles) north

Entry prices

Entry into Gobustan, Yanar Dag and Ateshgah of Baku are all very affordable. A ticket for Gobustan National Park starts at 4 AZN (£1.90) for locals and 10 AZN (£4.70) for foreigners, with an option of an excursion service at an extra cost. Yanar Dag costs 2 AZN (95p) for locals and 9 AZN (£4.30) for foreigners, and a combo ticket, which allows entry into both Yanar Dag and Ateshgah of Baku, costs 11 AZN (£5.20).

of Baku in the small village of Mahammadli.

Local lore is that the flames were ignited when a shepherd tossed a cigarette here in the 1950s. Natural gas leaks, caused by tectonic shifts and volcanic activity below the surface of the Earth, have kept the flames constantly ablaze since, regardless of the weather. However, when Venetian explorer Marco Polo visited Baku in the 13th century, during his travels of Central Asia, he cited the blazing, natural fires of the region in his memoirs; he was most likely referring to Yanar Dag.

The **Yanar Dag Museum** opened at this site in June 2019 and includes video installations and 3D layouts teaching visitors about the significance of fire and Zoroastrianism in Azerbaijan, as well as the mud volcanoes in the southwest of Baku. Exhibitions include 'Shadow of Forgotten Ancestors' by Azerbaijani artist Huseyn Hagverdiyev and 'Miracle of Light and Shadows.' Outside, try your hand at Gaval Dash (Qavaldaş), a large rock that when bashed with a stone, would make a musical sound. It was used in ancient times to notify tribes that there was a death in the village or an animal had been hunted and killed. If you can't get here by car, there's a four-hour tour departing from Freedom Square (next to

Park Bulvar Mall) at 11am and 4pm daily for 25 AZN (£12) per person.

BEACHES

Despite Baku's location by the Caspian Sea, there aren't as many public beaches as you would expect due to the high levels of oil pollution. But half an hour northeast in Baku's Sabunchi district is the settlement of **Bilgah**, home to one of Baku's cleanest beaches – a hit with the locals. Entry to the beach is free, but you will need to pay for the umbrella and chairs, and there are a handful of places dotted around for eating.

The Bilgah area is also home to the popular **Amburan Beach Club** ③ (www.amburan.com; daily 10am–11pm), which offers

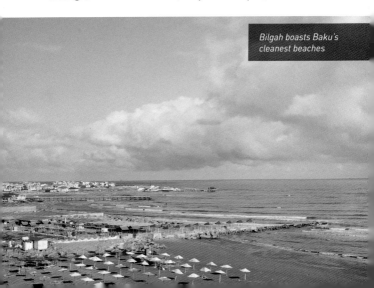

Bilgah boasts Baku's cleanest beaches

beach access, pools, restaurants and the five-star Bilgah Beach Hotel (formerly a Jumeirah property).

Another favourite with locals is Shikhov Beach in the southwest of Baku (as long as you don't mind the redundant oil rigs in the background). There is also a water park near here and the family-friendly Mambo Beach Club & Restaurant (Salyan Highway; tel: 55-455 0522; www.mambobeach.az). Five minutes on foot is the upmarket Crescent Beach Hotel (tel: 12-497 4777; www.cbh.az), the first beach resort on Baku's coast.

Note that all beach resorts charge entry for non-guests. Hiring a car or getting a taxi are the best transport

⊙ A CITY OF STILTS

Neft Daşları (Neft Daşları, meaning Oil Rocks in Azerbaijani), is the world's first offshore oil platform and a man-made city built entirely out at sea. Located in the Khazar raion it was built in the Caspian Sea in 1949 to house oilmen after oil was discovered in the region. It is situated around 100km (62 miles) from the coast of Baku, spanning across 300km (186 miles) of elevated road.

In its heyday, the 'floating city' was equipped to house 5,000 people with high-rise apartments, a bakery, laundrette and even its own football pitch. Since the collapse of the Soviet Union and the discovery of oil elsewhere in the area, the condition of the city is said to be slowly deteriorating. Getting permission to visit is virtually impossible, and the site doesn't even appear on Google maps. However, the unusual site was featured in the 1999 James Bond film, *The World Is Not Enough.*

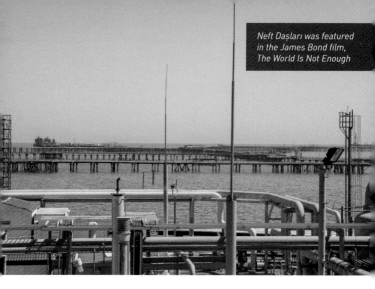

Neft Daşları was featured in the James Bond film, The World Is Not Enough

options, but both beaches can be reached using public transport too; bus 125 takes roughly one hour from Baku Puppet Theatre and takes you to within a 10 minute walk of Shikhov, and for Bilgah, take the 186 bus from Ulduz then change to the 171. Once you reach your destination, do as the locals do and order a plate of cold watermelon with a side of salted cheese; a great way to cool down in sweltering temperatures.

NATIONAL PARKS

Azerbaijan is home to eight national parks, all diverse in climate, landscape and wildlife. Some can be visited as part of a day trip from Baku. Around 63km (39 miles) east of the city centre is **Absheron National Park** ❿, a vast stretch of remote land right on the 'beak' of the Absheron Peninsula. The nature reserve, 7.8 sq km (3 sq miles) in size, was created in 1969

Local superstitions

One of Azerbaijan's most peculiar superstitions takes place at the Pir Hasan Sanctuary in Mardakan, where locals have bottles smashed over their heads in a bid to cure them of nerves.

in a bid to protect the seals, gazelles and water birds that inhabit the area.

Shirvan National Park ⓸, in the city of Salyan around 138km (86 miles) south of Baku, is a gem for nature and wildlife lovers, with 0.6 sq km (0.2 sq miles) of semi-desert land that's home to the rare and endangered goitered gazelles, as well as 14 species of birds and flamingos who gather at Flamingo Lake come autumn and winter. Other animals to keep an eye out for include foxes, jackals, wolves and lizards. Ophidiophobes beware, it's not uncommon to see a number of non-poisonous snakes in both these areas.

The national park is also home to three mud volcanoes, the most prominent being Bandovan Mountain. Entry here costs just 2 AZN (90p), and there is the option to stay in one of the wooden lodges in the park.

Getting to both of these places is difficult unless you have a car, and, even then, there is a lack of information and signposts, so your best option is an organised tour. Azerbaijan-Tours (10 Huseyn Cavid Avenue; tel: 70-202 7040; www.azerbaijan-tours.com) offers day tours, available by request, and will take you from Baku to both Absheron and Shirvan national parks accompanied by an English-speaking guide. A return trip from Baku to Absheron costs $150 (£120) and to Shirvan $200 (£160), regardless of the number of people in the group. They also offer private transfer services across Baku and the rest of the country.

FAR EAST AND THE ABSHERON PENINSULA

Further east of Baku and around the Absheron Peninsula are small settlements and villages that portray the most unruffled, traditional way of life; chances are you will pass through a few during day trips in this area. If simplicity is your thing, it's worth stopping in a couple of these, but beware, the people here are not terribly accustomed to tourists, so be sensitive, especially when taking photos, and avoid talking loudly.

Ramana, in the Subunchi raion of Baku, is one of the oldest villages in Baku, and is said to have been founded by the Romans. In the late 19th/early 20th century, it was known for producing mass amounts of industrial oil. **Ramana Castle** ㊷ is well worth a visit, where you can climb to the top and observe the entirety of this sleepy and traditional village. The key to the castle is held

Shirvan National Park

Mardakan Castle

by a woman who lives next door, so opening hours can be tentative.

Further east (around 20km/12 miles) is the open-air **Archaeological and Ethnographic Museum Complex** (9am–6pm daily) in the village of Qala. Sprawled across the complex are monuments (some ancient, some replicas), houses and activities like bread baking and iron forging.

Mardakan, another one of the Absheron Peninsula's oldest villages, is situated in the Khazar raion and is located 12km (7 miles) north of Qala (or a 12km (7-mile) drive east if you are coming from the airport). Here you will find traditional, metal-gated houses, the Pir Hasan sanctuary, where philanthropist Haji Zeynalabdin Taghiyev is buried, and the 12th-century quadrilingual **Mardakan Castle** ⓸ (Dördkünc Mərdəkan Qalası; tel: 50-722 7234; daily 9am–7pm). The 22 metre (72ft) -high, five-tiered castle here was built by Akhsitan I, the 21st king of the Shirvan dynasty, who is most known for moving the capital from Shamakhi to Baku. It's possible to climb to the top for panoramic views of the area, but be aware that the steps are narrow and the grounds in general are unrepaired. Also, bear in mind that the gatekeeper doesn't speak any English, so bring an Azeri/Russian-speaking friend if you can. According to reports in 2019, there are plans for a renovation. Bus 136 from Koroglu Metro Station will bring you within walking distance.

Neighbouring **Shuvalan**, 4km (2.5 miles) east of Mardakan, is home to **Mir Movsum Aga Mosque** 🄴 (daily 24 hours), a shrine dedicated to Mir Movsum Aga, who was considered to have supernatural powers and thought to have healed people just by the touch of his hand. The interior of the double-domed, Central Asian-style mosque is covered in thousands of glittering mosaic tiles.

Approximately 7km (4.3 miles) north from here is Dalga Beach Aquapark Resort, one of the country's largest water parks. Other nearby villages include **Nardaran** (reached via Bilgah), one of the most religiously conservative areas in the country and home to a 12th-century fortress built by architect Mahmud ibn Sa'ad. The village also hosts the annual International Musical Festival Zhara (www.zhara.az) every summer at the Sea Breeze Resort.

Inside Mir Movsum Aga Mosque

Souvenirs sold at a local market in the Old City of Baku (Icheri Sheher)

WHAT TO DO

SHOPPING

Baku has a mishmash of everything when it comes to shopping. Both **Nizami Street** and **Neftchilar Avenue** are lined with local and international designer shops, including the likes of Gucci and Dior, and the last decade has sprouted impressive new shopping centres like the swanky **Port Baku Mall** and the multi-storey **Park Bulvar**. But the city's most endearing shopping experiences lies in its buzzy outdoor bazaars and roadside souvenir shops, where you can pick up anything from a traditional kilim rug to a bag of apples sold from the boot of an old Lada.

MARKETS

Baku's wealth of bazaars are one of the city's most charming and authentic draws. Aromatic, colourful, and thronging with shouting stall owners, they have been an integral part of daily life for generations. The city's largest is **Taza Bazar** (Təzə Bazar; daily 8am–7pm) on Samad Vurgun Street, not too far from 28 May Station. It's also one of the city's oldest, and sells almost everything, including fruits and vegetables, spices, caviar, pickles, cheese, meat, fish (beware, the fish here is pungent) and household products.

Yashil Bazar (Yaşıl Bazar; daily 6am–10pm) on Khatai Avenue, known as Green Market, is another popular bazaar among Bakuvians, mainly indoors but with a small outdoor section where cabbages and watermelons are sold from the back of a lorry.

Two kilometres (1.2 miles) northeast of here, past the zoo, will take you to **Nasimi Bazar**, where you'll find almost anything from organic fruits and fresh flowers to cookware and

Azeri carpets for sale

crockery. In the Narimanov raion is **Keshla Bazar** (Keşlə Bazar; daily 6am– 10pm), not well known among tourists but a great place for picking up affordable local delicacies such as *lavashana* (sheets of pressed, sour plum), multiple flavours of *mürəbbə* (sweet fruit preserve). You can also buy *üzərlik*, a dried plant that is believed to keep evil spirits away.

Those seeking an even more hyper-local experience can head to the 'Russian Bazar' in the city's Subunchu raion, a local flea market that was birthed to make extra money during the rule of the Soviet Union. It's a sprawling mix of old clothes, shoes and pots and pans. Don't expect any of the stall owners to speak any English; you may be surprised how far you can get with hand gestures.

In the heart of Baku, the **Old City** is sprinkled with colourful shops and markets selling traditional rugs and Soviet-era memorabilia, as well as the expected magnets, trinkets and postcards.

CARPETS AND ANTIQUES

You do not have to spend long in Baku to realise that the city has an impenetrable love affair with carpets. Rug fiends should head to the rustic Old City where carpets abound. You will see them draped over the bonnets of rusty Ladas and displayed in masses at roadside shops like Flying Carpets and Brothers Carpets; note that most shops do not have names. Beware that not all of the carpets are authentic and some are produced in China or Iran. Azeri carpets are mostly made using sheep's wool, and use the colours red, blue, green, yellow and cream. The most common types are 'kilim' and 'soumak'. Sellers here are used to bartering, so it's worth learning a few phrases in Azerbaijani to try and reduce the price.

ART AND HANDICRAFTS

Armudu glasses

Azeris drink their tea from a glass called *armudu*, which means 'pear-shaped'. These traditional glasses are available to buy from most Old City souvenir shops, ranging from mass-produced budget-friendly options to those that are hand glazed using the traditional buta pattern. Prices for a single *armudu* ranges from 5 to 150 manats, depending on the material and quality.

⊘ EXPORT CERTIFICATE

Remember, you can only take an antique product (including carpets, art, samovars and copperware) out of the country if it was made after 1960, and even then, you will require an export certificate from the Ministry of Culture/relevant museum (www.mct.gov.az). These can be issued from the Azerbaijan Carpet Museum for carpets and rugs, the National Art Museum for any artwork, the Azerbaijan State Museum of Musical Culture for musical instruments and the National Library of Azerbaijan for manuscripts. Permit prices vary according to item size and year of production.

Naftalan paintings

Art lovers looking for a one-of-a-kind piece should head to the studio of artist **Sabir Chopuroghlu** (92 Mirmahmud Kazimovski Street), who uses the country's famous Naftalan crude oil to paint scenes of Baku, and even takes commissions for personalised paintings. You can find similar paintings made with Naftalan oil dotted around the small shops in the Old City.

Silk scarves

Another one of Azerbaijan's most prized products is its handmade silk scarves using natural dyes, known locally as kelagayi – a practice enlisted in Unesco's List of Intangible Cultural Heritage in 2014. Local designer **Menzer Hajiyeva** (www.menzerhajiyeva.com) specialises in scarves and prints. She also launched a programme in 2016 to train local women to become kelagayi artisans in a bid to promote and preserve the unique craft. Make an appointment to swing by her pretty studio at 31 Aziz Aliyev Street, near Gosha Gala Gapisi, to buy yourself, or a friend, a unique gift from Azerbaijan.

Silk scarves for sale in Baku's Old City

Backgammon boards

Old men and backgammon are synonymous in Baku. A handful of shops in the Old City sell handmade wooden backgammon sets that are either plain or painted – with traditional patterns or with Baku's emblems such as the beloved Maiden Tower.

ENTERTAINMENT

Tickets for theatre shows, concerts and any other events can be found at www.iticket.az. Be aware that most theatre shows and film showings are in either Azerbaijani or Russian, with the odd one offering English subtitles.

THEATRE AND OPERA

Theatre culture is strong in Baku, ranging from the grandiose opera house to puppet theatres tucked away in small alleyways. One of the most iconic theatres is the 600-seater **Azerbaijan State Academic Opera and Ballet Theater** (see page 55) on Nizami Street, where you can catch classical plays and dance performances, mostly by Azerbaijani artists. Both **Baku Puppet Theatre** (77 Neftchilar Avenue) and **Baku Marionette Theatre** (20 Muslim Magpmayev Street; www.marionet.az) perform all their shows in either Azerbaijani or Russian, but the simplicity of the storylines make them easy for tourists to follow.

For music lovers, both the **Rashid Behbudov State Song Theatre** (12 Rashid Behbudov Street) and the ornate **Azerbaijan State Musical Theatre** (8 Zarifa Aliyeva Street) put on regular performances of traditional musical styles, such as folk and mugham, by national composers like Uzeyir Hajibeyov. The latter is one of the oldest theatres in the country. The **Azerbaijan State Pantomime Theatre** (www.pantomima.az) on Azadliq Avenue is housed inside a former chapel, and puts on an array of creative mime performances of various themes. The best part is you do not need to speak Azerbaijani to enjoy the show.

Other notable theatres include the **Azerbaijan State Russian Drama Theater** on Khagani Street and **Azerbaijan State Academic National Drama Theatre** at the end of Fuzuli Park. Fully restored in 2005, the 2,500 seater **Yashil Theatre** (tel: 12-492 26 37), near the Flame Towers, is a great sea-facing amphitheatre that puts on a variety of shows. Finding a show schedule is not easy, so either call for information or check www.iticket.az.

CINEMA AND MUSIC

The multi-screen **Nizami Cinema Center**, built in 1940, is the oldest cinema in Baku, and shows films in Azeri, Turkish and Russian. For cinephiles wanting to make the most of Baku's balmy evenings, there are a couple of outdoor cinema options. **Baku Open Air Cinema** (daily 8pm–3am) is an independent cinema on the western end of the boulevard in the city's Bayil District. This sea-facing venue features a sky-high screen showing a mix of film classics and new releases. Tickets are only 5 AZN and can be purchased on the spot. The brand new **AIRWE open-air cinema** at Luna Park on Nobel Avenue shows films Monday to Thursday, with cushioned seating and food and drink trucks. Information regarding shows and timings can be found on their Instagram page, airwebaku. **Park Cinema**, inside the boulevard's Park Bulvar shopping centre has a schedule of films in English, Azeri and Russian. There are four Park Cinema branches in the city, including one at the Flame Towers.

The city's main concert venues are **Heydar Aliyev Palace** and **Baku Crystal Hall**, the latter playing host to the Eurovision Song Contest and international superstar performances for the Azerbaijan Grand Prix.

Lovers of jazz should head to Baku in October, when the city hosts the annual **Baku Jazz Festival** (www.bakujazzfestival.

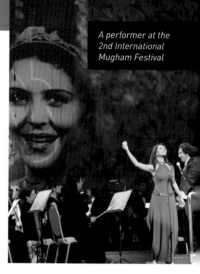

A performer at the 2nd International Mugham Festival

com) with a 10-day programme of live performances, exhibitions and workshops across multiple venues in the city. For jazz year-round, the intimate **Blue Moon Jazz Cafe** (79 Mirza Mansur) in the Old City has local performers every evening, or for something a little more upmarket, there is also the **The Jazz Club** at Fairmont Baku Flame Towers. The **Friends of Jazz** (5 Nariman Narimanov Avenue; www. jazz.az), formerly the Baku Jazz Center on Rashid Behbudov Street, is the newly-launched union of jazz performers, focussing on promoting and nurturing Azerbaijani jazz.

Azerbaijan's most famous jazz musician is Vagif Mustafazadeh, known for fusing jazz with the country's beloved traditional musical style, mugham. His house is now a museum in the Old City (see page 36). For current jazz events and tickets, head to www.citylife.az.

Mugham

Mugham (*muğam*), Azerbaijan's treasured, melancholic musical expression is integral to the country's identity, so much so that in 2003, Unesco declared it a 'Masterpiece of Oral and Intangible Heritage of the World'. The genre is an expression of sorrow and longing, and is usually improvisational, consisting of three musicians; a singer (known as a *xanəndə*), who's usually holding a percussion instrument called *qaval*, and two instrumentalists (a *sazəndə*) playing the traditional string instruments *tar* and *kamança*. A performance of mugham is a must for a taste of authentic Azerbaijan, and there are a handful of venues in the city that specialise in it.

The **International Mugham Center** (9 Neftchilar Avenue) on the boulevard is dedicated to preserving the art of mugham and hosts regular concerts and workshops. **Mugam Klub** (see page 110) restaurant, housed inside a former caravanserai in the Old City puts on nightly performances to accompany the delicious traditional dinner served. The country's most famous mugham singer is Alim Qasimov, who was awarded the Unesco International Music Council Music Prize in 1999. Many of the city's theatres also put on regular mugham performances.

NIGHTLIFE

Baku's nightlife ranges from multi-storey nightclubs to hipster-chic cosy wine bars, although the former are not very popular with the city's young, creative folk. Come night-time, most locals flock to Fountains Square or the Bulvar, which offer a multitude of places to drink and socialise. Beware: a number of clubs and bars have been known to deny entry to single males, and there is almost always an entry charge for the larger clubs.

Barrel Playground on the west end of the Bulvar is a lively open-air club and a relatively new concept for Baku's nightlife. Expect creative cocktails, themed DJ sets and performances of techno, electro and jazz. Open seasonally. For those looking for something a bit more upbeat, clubs **Otto** on Abdulakarim Alizadeh Street, **Enerji** on National Flag Square and the South American-themed **Pacifico** on Neftchilar Avenue all start to gather crowds from around 1am onwards.

Around Fountains Square, the art-focussed **ROOM** on Tarlan Aliyarbeyov Street is Baku's answer to a Shoreditch-style wine joint, and is perfect for avoiding the typical, tourist-centric bars. It stays open until 4am and serves up great local and international wines and appetisers. Live jazz and blues performances are also a feature. Surprisingly, there is also an Irish bar here, **Finnegans**, which serves Guinness and hosts regular live bands.

For beer lovers, the upmarket yet relaxed **BeerBasha** (8A Parliament Avenue; www.beat.az) restaurant (with an on-site microbrewery), a short funicular ride from the city centre, stays open until 2am, and serves up some of the best beer in town. There is a selection of pale and dark beers and ales and a snack menu including seafood, fries and German-style sausages on offer. For cheaper beer, head to the cylindrical-shaped **Camel Pub and Cafe** (191 Bashir Safaroglu Street).

The dive bar-esque **Le Chateau Music Bar** on Islam Safarli Street is popular with hip 20-somethings, and offers live gigs and a beer for as little as 1 AZN. Fancier clubs include **Eleven** lounge/club (on the 11th floor of Park Inn hotel, 1 Azadliq Avenue) which comes with glittering city views. The pan-Asian **CHINAR** (1 Shovkat Alakbarova Street) is Baku's answer to Soho House, and this is where you are likely to spot local celebrities. It gets really busy at weekends, so be sure to book a table on the terrace to sit back and enjoy the resident DJ's mellow playlist.

The European Games 2015 were held in Baku

Try to spend at least one evening aimlessly strolling the boulevard and people-watching at Fountains Square, indulging in some tea and sweets at a street-side café; a favourite evening pastime of Bakuvians.

SPORTS

SPECTATOR SPORTS

Baku's potential as a sports tourism destination has grown rapidly in recent years. Although freestyle wrestling has traditionally been the national sport, football is undoubtedly more popular. The main teams in Baku are Neftchi Baku, FC Baku and Keshla FK.

By far the biggest stadium is the 68,700-seater **Baku Olympic Stadium** (www.bos.az), slightly east of the city centre near Boyukshore Lake. The world-class venue, which opened in 2015, is where the national team play most of their home games. It hosted the UEFA Europa League Final in 2019 and will host group matches and the quarter final for the UEFA Euro championship in the spring of 2020. For avid football fans, there are hour-long guided tours available in English, Azerbaijani, Russian and German, which can be arranged via submission on the website.

Tofiq Bahramov Republican Stadium (see page 70), also in the east, served as the home ground of the Azerbaijani national team until the opening of Baku Olympic Stadium, although some national games are still played here. It's named after Tofiq Bahramov, the referee who played a pivotal role in England's 1966 World Cup victory against West Germany. The 1951 stadium was also the home ground of the Premier League side Qarabag FK until they moved to **Azersun Arena**, further east in the Suraxani raion.

Qarabag FK is originally from the city of Agdam in south-west Azerbaijan, but they have played in Baku since 1993 when Agdam became victim of the Nagorno-Karabakh war and fell into Armenian hands. **Bakcell Arena** in the Nizami raion is the home stadium of rival team Neftchi Baku. For more information on Azerbaijani football, head to www.affa.az, home of the Association of Football Federations of Azerbaijan.

Notable multi-sport competitions to be hosted in Baku include the 2015 European Games and the 2019 European Youth Olympic Festival, as well as the annual Azerbaijan Grand

⊘ PRECURSOR OF POLO

Chovqan, named after the wooden mallet used to play it, is a traditional horseback sport that dates back thousands of years. The game, enlisted in Unesco's List of Intangible Cultural Heritage in Need of Urgent Safeguarding, is traditionally played on Karabakh horses, Azerbaijan's cherished national animal. The aim is to get the leather ball into the opponent's goal using the mallet. Traditional uniform consists of a papakha (wooly hat), arkhalig (jacket) and trousers. The Republican Equestrian Tourism Center in the city of Sheki hosts the annual chovqan competition to celebrate the sport that was considered aristocratic since ancient times.

Prix, held in Baku since 2017. The city has bid twice to host the Summer Olympics, both of which were unsuccessful.

PARTICIPANT SPORTS

Baku's leading golf course is Dreamland Golf Club (www.dreamlandgolfclub.com) just by Zigh Highway, around 26km (16 miles) east of central Baku. The 18-hole championship golf course offers lessons, tee time and private hire for non-members. There are a handful of clean and safe public beaches along Baku's coast for a spot of swimming, including the popular Bilgah and Shikhov (see page 79).

ACTIVITIES FOR CHILDREN

Baku has plenty of public play areas and spacious parks for children to run wild, including the Bulvar, Central Park and the ever-popular Fountains Square, which is home to a vintage-style carousel. Children-focussed parks with playgrounds and kids activities include Port Baku Kids Park on the east end of Neftchilar Avenue, Koala Park (daily 10am–11pm) on Azadliq Avenue and Baku Zoological Park just next door.

The city's main waterpark, Dalga Beach Aqua Park Resort, offers a kids club and those aged six and under can enter for free. On the boulevard, kids will love Tusi Bohm Planetarium (www.planetarium.az; Mon–Fri 5–8pm, Sat–Sun 1–8pm) on the 4th floor of Park Bulvar shopping centre, where the entire family can enjoy a virtual tour of the planet, equipped with a 4K 10-metre screen showing films, cartoons and educational documentaries. On the floor below is HappyLand (www.happylandfun.az; daily 10am–8pm), another kids' paradise with games, amusement rides and a toy shop.

CALENDAR OF EVENTS

Novruz. March 20–24. The biggest holiday in the country celebrating the coming of spring, accompanied by street ceremonies.

International World of Mugham Festival. March. A week-long festival celebrating mugham music with concerts and contests.

Azerbaijan Grand Prix. Usually April or June. The international racing competition comes to Baku.

Caspian Oil and Gas Show. June. A large international trade fair.

Baku Street Food Festival. June/July. A three-week food festival with music, masterclasses and food from restaurants around the city.

UEFA Euro Quarter Finals 2020. 4 July. Baku Olympic Stadium will play host to group matches and the quarter finals. www.uefa.com.

Zhara. July. A four-day music festival in Nardaran featuring artists mainly from Azerbaijan and Russia. www.zhara.az.

Baku International Book Fair. September. Publishers from around the world gather at Baku Sports Palace.

Nasimi Festival. September/October. A festival launched in 2019 to celebrate revered poet Imadeddin Nasimi. See www.nasimifestival.live for programmes.

Baku International Jazz Festival. October. A week-long festival with gigs and events at venues across the city. See www.bakujazzfestival.com.

MAP Festival. October/November. A performing arts festival, taking place across various Baku theatres. www.mapfestival.az.

Baku International Tourism Film Festival. November. The Nizami International Cinema Centre plays host to this non-profit festival that celebrates local and international films which promote tourism.

EATING OUT

Diving into the food culture is paramount to exploring Baku. Azerbaijani food is rich, fresh and aromatic, and although it's little-known outside of the Caucasus region, it's a gastronome's dream. The cuisine is a unique mix of dishes that are unequivocally local, with Turkish, Persian and Russian influences, all of which culminate in the capital's culinary scene.

Restaurants vary from the rug-clad, medieval caravanserais in the Old City that serve some of the best kebabs in town, to plush, rooftop fine-dining affairs that come with dress codes and universal menus. Vegetarians, beware. Meat-free options aren't as advanced here as in European cities, but some restaurants offer alternatives like vegetable kebabs and fresh salads.

The quintessential menu consists of different types of grilled kebab, pilaf dishes, stuffed vegetables and vine leaves, ground meat, soups and lots of fresh fruits and greens. Larger dishes like *plov* (pilau) or those made in a *saj* (large skillet) are placed in the centre of the table for everyone to share.

SOUPS, STARTERS AND SIDES

Soups are a little different here, and tend to be thicker and more concentrated. Local soups include *dovğa*, consisting of yoghurt with herbs, which can be ordered as cold or warm soup, or as a refreshing drink.

Piti is cooked inside individual clay pots and placed in a special stove in the wall. It is made with mutton and vegetables and infused with saffron water for colour and flavour. Originally it came from the ancient city of Sheki in the northwest; some traditional restaurants in Baku serve up their own variation.

Küftə bozbaş is a local stew-like meatball soup, cooked in an aromatic broth of potatoes and chickpeas. The beetroot-rich *borscht*, originally from Russia (although the Ukrainians might beg to differ), is another regular on menus in Baku, and particularly popular during winter.

Düşbərə is a popular dumpling soup, offered in most local restaurants, made with little parcels of dough filled with lamb or beef and cooked in a broth of onion, spices and salt, seasoned with dried mint. Due to their heaviness, soups can also be served as main courses.

Dovğa is a local soup

Fresh salads make favoured side dishes, and include *mangal* with grilled aubergines, peppers and tomatoes; *çoban* with tomatoes, cucumbers, onion and bell peppers; and Russian salad with eggs, potatoes, carrots, meat and mayonnaise.

It's normal for restaurants in Baku to serve you a plate of fresh, raw vegetables and herbs as an appetizer. This usually consists of raw onion, herbs (mostly tarragon), cucumbers and tomatoes. Order a side of pickles, too, which will complement just about everything on the menu.

BREAD

Bread, or *çörək*, is sacred here, so much so that it's frowned upon to throw any of it away, and if you see any on the floor, you must pick it up. It's eaten for breakfast, lunch and dinner. It's normal to have a piece of bread on the side of each meal. Restaurants usually bring a basket of bread, even if you don't ask for it.

Təndir bread, made using a traditional clay oven in the ground, is what Baku does best, and you can even watch it being baked in a few of the humble restaurants in the Old City.

You shouldn't leave Baku without trying *qutab,* a thin flatbread stuffed with cheese and spinach. There are a few 'it' places in the Old City (see page 29) that specialise in *qutab,* with prices starting from just 1 AZN per portion. Fillings can vary, depending on the restaurant, but most typically include cottage cheese, coriander, dill, pumpkin, meat and onions.

If there isn't one already on the table, ask for a small pot of sumac to sprinkle over the *qutab;* this is how the locals eat it.

To try *fəsəli,* a flaky flatbread that comes either plain or spiced, head to Kichik Gala Street in the Old City, where old ladies make and sell it on the side of the road.

MEAT

Most Bakuvians are carnivores, with lamb, chicken and beef dominating menus around the city. Kebabs are synonymous with the typical Baku dinner table, and all local restaurants will dish up different varieties. The most popular one is *şaşlik;*

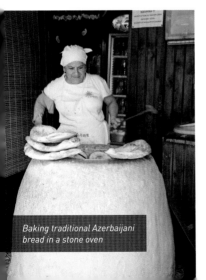

Baking traditional Azerbaijani bread in a stone oven

skewers of lamb or chicken cubes grilled over a charcoal fire, and served with a fresh and herbaceous salad. *Lülə* kebabs are made using minced meat, onions and lumps of fat, and *tava* kebabs are round cutlets of lamb cooked in a frying pan. Most menus will also feature sturgeon kebab; these are a bit more expensive. Kebabs tend to be served with a side of rice and fresh salad, as well as pickles and a garnish of pungent, raw onion.

> ### Cheers!
>
> 'Nuş olsun!' is the expression used right before eating, the equivalent of 'bon appetite!'. Before drinking, it's either the Azeri 'sağlığına' meaning 'to your health', or the Russian 'nazdarovya'.

Other popular meat dishes include the ubiquitous dolma, which consists of meat, rice and herbs stuffed inside either vine leaves or vegetables like peppers, tomatoes, cabbage or aubergine. The dish's name comes from the Azerbaijani word for 'filling' and there are around 25 different variations.

Xəngəl is a simple but delicious dish consisting of a bed of square pasta pieces with minced meat and onion, often eaten with a dollop of garlic yoghurt on the side. You're also bound to see *qovurma* on the menu, a lamb stew available in many different varieties.

RICE

There are around 40 types of *plov* (sometimes called *aş*), Azerbaijan's much-loved, saffron-infused signature rice dish. Each region of the country has its own variation, which include *şah* (lamb with dried fruit and nuts), *toyug* (chicken) and *qoyun* (mutton). Another popular one is Baku's speciality, *səbzi plov*, made with lamb and coriander, dill, leek, spinach and sorrel, and cooked using lots and lots of butter. You will find this in

most traditional restaurants
in the city, each perfecting it
in a slightly different way.
Like all *plovs*, it's made to
serve around four or five
people, and no celebration,
however big or small, is
complete without it.

FISH

Fish lovers rejoice — Baku's
location next to the Caspian
Sea enriches its restau-
rants with some of the tastiest fish around. Fish is often served
with either a plum sauce, *lavaşana turşu*, or a thick, pomegranate sauce, *narşərab*.

The most common types of fish are beluga sturgeon and
Caspian kutum, and local menus include dishes like *baliq
ləvəngi* (fish stuffed with walnuts and fruit sauce); various sturgeon dishes; fish pilau and salmon.

The city also has a couple of fish-focussed restaurants, located
around the coast slightly away from the city centre. Shellfish is
not particularly popular here, you are more likely to find prawns
and scallops on more contemporary and international menus.

Beluga caviar, once abundant in Bakuvian households, became
more expensive after the collapse of the Soviet Union. Today, you
can find it in outdoor markets like Taza Bazar, in speciality shops
all around the city and on menus in upmarket restaurants.

ALCOHOL

Azerbaijan is a secular state, so alcohol is widely sold in
shops and served in the majority of cafés and restaurants in

Baku. Research shows that winemaking started somewhere in the Caucasus region thousands of years ago, and although Azerbaijani wine often falls under the shadow of neighbouring Georgia, you will find a good selection of local red and white wines in most Baku restaurants, with the majority being semi-dry and dry. The country's speciality is pomegranate wine, but this isn't sold everywhere.

There are no vineyards in Baku. Key wine-making regions in the country include Ağsu, Gabala, Shamkir, Ganja and Göygöl. Wine in restaurants can be ordered by the glass or bottle, and bottle prices range between 15 AZN and 45 AZN. The city now has a small number of wine bars and also a guided 'wine crawl' to please even the most seasoned oenophile.

NON-ALCOHOLIC DRINKS

Non-alcoholic drinks are just as popular on a typical Baku menu. The most common ones include feijoa compote, a syruppy juice made using the feijoa fruit; ayran, a salty yoghurt drink; dovğa, another yoghurt drink with herbs which can also be consumed as a soup; and, of course, the nation's favourite, tea. Most juices come in glasses or, more commonly, in a jug for the whole table.

Azerbaijani wines

DESSERT, PASTRIES AND SWEETS

Dessert is just as important as the main course in Azerbaijan, and, in most cases, wildly sugary and calorific. Almost always consumed with a *çay* (tea), the most popular sweets include *paxlava*, a multi-layered, diamond-shaped pastry filled with sugar, nuts and honey; *şəkərbura*, a crescent-shaped pastry filled with ground nuts, sugar, honey and a touch of cardamom and fresh fruit like watermelon and figs.

Pastries are particularly popular during Novruz, the coming

⊘ TEA CULTURE

Tea is woven into the DNA of Azerbaijanis, who drink it strong and in copious amounts. Locals drink it black with a slice of lemon, and it's usually served in an armudu, a pear-shaped glass that cools the top layer of tea while keeping the bottom hot. To sweeten it, a sugar cube is usually dunked in tea and bitten off. Alternatively, it is drunk with a spoon of *mürəbbə*, a runny fruit preserve. There is usually an accompanying glass container full of chocolates and sweets, too.

Traditionally, tea is served out of a samovar, a metal container used to boil and dispense water, which became popular during Russian occupancy. A *çayxana*, meaning 'tea house', is an important part of daily, traditional life, and there are a few of them dotted around in Baku, like the charming Old Baku Tea House or Çay Evi 145 on Neftchilar Avenue.

Coffee culture is only recently becoming somewhat popular in Baku, and there were a few eyebrows raised when the very first Starbucks opened in the city back in 2015. If you are desperate for a coffee hit, head to the trendy, movie-themed Coffee Moffie behind Fountains Square.

Azerbaijani tea served in an armudu

of spring and the country's main national holiday. You might find cake on menus, but it's not popular with locals, unless it's at a wedding or a special celebration. If you don't have much of a sweet tooth, opt for a non-savoury pastry like *şorgogal*, an aromatic bun with caraway seeds. Some restaurants also offer halva, but Baku halva is very different to the solidified, nutty kind of the Middle East. Here, it's almost like caramel, with a runny, sugary texture.

CHEESE

The most intense-flavoured cheese is *motal*, a hard, white crumbly cheese made from goat's milk and matured inside a sheepskin. In the more low-key, traditional restaurants, you can order a small slice of *motal* on its own, or as part of a cheeseboard with the likes of feta and other hard cheeses.

A summertime favourite among Bakuvians is snacking on *təndir* bread, cold watermelon and feta-like white cheese on a hot summer's day.

INTERNATIONAL CUISINE

Restaurants specialising in international cuisine have only recently emerged in Baku. There are a small handful around the city centre, including French, Indian and Japanese.

TO HELP YOU ORDER

Do you have a table? **Boş yeriniz var?**
The bill, please **Hesabi getirin zəhmət olmasa**
I would like... **Mən istəyərdim...**
I am a vegetarian/vegan... **Mən vegetarianam/veganam**
I am allergic to... **Allergiyam var**

tea **çay**	salt **duz**
coffee **qəhvə**	pepper **istiot**
bread **çörək**	vegetables **tərəvəzlər**
butter **yağ**	fruit **meyvə**
milk **süd**	ice-cream **dondurma**
sugar **şəkər**	jam **cem**
meat **ət**	water **su**
fish **balıq**	starters **qəlyalantılar**
beer **pivə**	dessert **desertlər**
soup **şorba**	rice **düyü**
wine **şərab**	drinks **içkilər**
cheese **pendir**	juice **şirə**
salad **salat**	

MENU READER

kebab **kabab**	nuts **qoz-fındıq**
lamb **quzu**	plum **gavalı**
chicken **toyuq**	prawns **karides**
beef **mal əti**	pickles **turşu**
pomegranate **nar**	pepper **bibar**
onion **soğan**	cake **tort**
aubergine **badımcan**	yoghurt **qatıq**
garlic **sarımsaq**	stew **güveç**
potatoes **kartoflar**	pastry **xəmir**
herbs **otlar**	sheep **qoyun**
cabbage **kələm**	chestnut **şabalıd**

PLACES TO EAT

The prices are an indication for a two-course meal for one, with either a soft drink or a local beer. It excludes service charge, which is usually 5–10 percent. *Saj* dishes, consisting of a large pan of meat, vegetables and potatoes made for sharing, tend to be more expensive. Unless stated, the restaurants listed here accept credit card.

££££	over £25
£££	£15–25
££	£10–15
£	under £10

ICHERI SHEHER (OLD CITY)

Burc Qala Restaurant ££ *15 Kichik Gala Street; tel: 50-227 0090. Open Mon–Fri 9am–11pm, Sat–Sun 8am–11pm.* Slightly hipster, slightly traditional, this haunt is part of the Old City walls and has a delicious menu of regional dishes. Duck in here for breakfast or a light lunch of *qutab* with a generous sprinkling of sumac and the Azeri favourite, a platter of pickles. Outdoor seating available.

Han Restaurant £££ *22 Asaf Zeynalli Street; tel: 50-669 1331. Open daily 8–1am.* Through a wooden ogive door is this huge, 12th-century caravanserai-cum-restaurant that feels like a page out of an Azeri storybook. The menu serves up Azeri and Turkish dishes as well as mouth-watering steaks. If the central courtyard gets too busy, book one of the 10 cosy 'VIP' rooms decorated with works by local artists.

Le Kebab ££ *19 Sabir Street; tel: 12-492 7579. Open daily 9am–11pm.* Just off the main Kichik Gala Street, this casual chestnut-wood and stone joint is, as the name suggests, kebab gold. The fresh dishes here are beautifully presented and taste just as good. The helpful staff are happy to offer advice on how to spend the rest of your time in Baku.

Manqal ££ *126 Kichik Gala Street; tel: 50-803 7777. Open daily 10am–midnight.* Meat lovers rejoice. The name of this buzzy restaurant, located next to Qaynana, means 'barbecue' in Azeri. It lives up to this name with a menu packed full of delicious grilled lamb, chicken and fish. It also serves an equally fantastic *paxlava*. For an authentic lunch with atmosphere you can't go wrong with Manqal.

Mugam Klub ££££ *9 Hagigat Rzayeva Street; tel: 12-492 4085. Open daily 10am–midnight.* It would be a sin to leave Baku without eating here. A former two-storey caravanserai, this open-air, picture-perfect restaurant offers a menu of signature Azeri dishes like *sebzi plov* (lamb and rice with leek and herbs) and *qutab* (thin dough with spinach). Evenings here come with a performance of mugham — the nation's melancholic folk music. There are a handful of small souvenir shops on the floor above. Booking advised.

Qaynana Restaurant ££ *126 Kichik Gala Street; tel: 70-434 0013. Open daily 8am–midnight.* The name means 'mother-in-law' in Azeri, and it serves up some of the most authentic, humble fare in town. The *qutab* (rolled dough stuffed with cheese and spinach) here is to die for, and so is the lamb *buğlama* (stew). Service is efficient and friendly, and the background Azerbaijani music is a nice touch.

Qazmaq ££ *124 Kichik Gala Street; tel: 12-505 2226. Open daily 9am–midnight.* The terrace of this super-laid-back joint gets busy in the summer with revellers sipping on beer, tea or feijoa compote. There is an extensive menu, with breakfast, hot and cold dishes, local desserts and many, many drinks.

Sehrli Tendir £ *19 Kichik Gala Street; tel: 50-403 1435. Open daily 8am–11pm.* This low-key, rug-centric joint is one of the few places in Baku where locals will queue for lunch. Elderly women tirelessly bake bread using traditional *tendir* ovens. The menu never changes. Try dolma (stuffed vine leaves) with freshly-baked bread and a side of *motal* (hard goat cheese). Wash it down with *dovğa*, a yoghurt drink with herbs. Unbeatable value.

BOULEVARD AND NEFTCHILAR AVENUE

Atelier Vivanda £££ *153 Neftchilar Avenue; tel: 12-404 8204. Open Tue–Sun, noon–3pm, 5pm–midnight.* Michelin-starred French chef Akrame Benallal opened up this meat-focussed restaurant as part of Port Baku Mall, right on the boulevard. On the menu, expect thinly-sliced smoked beef that's been matured for 50 days, *pommes darphin* and an extra-large Angus steak. The set lunch menu is good value for money.

Cay Evi 145 ££ *115 Neftchilar Avenue; tel: 12-480 0019. Open daily 24 hours.* Near the eastern end of the boulevard, this rug-covered joint not only offers a long list of teas, as the name (tea house) suggests, but also a packed menu of Azeri and European dishes. It's particularly busy when football is broadcast on the big screen or there is a live band. Board games like backgammon and dominoes are available, and so is shisha.

Lalə Kafe £ *77 Neftchilar Avenue.* After dinner elsewhere, stop by this leafy, two-floor tea and pastry hangout just by Baku Puppet Theatre. The dimly lit lighting come evening makes it the perfect spot to while away time with a drink and something sweet. Unassuming, with outdoor seating available.

Paris Bistro ££ *1/4 Zarifa Aliyeva Street; tel: 12-404 8215. Open 24 hours.* A bit of an 'it' place among young Bakuvians, this trendy spot imitates Paris's ubiquitous stylish bistros. The park-facing, leafy terrace is perfect for a balmy morning. Get the honey-soaked French pancakes for breakfast or the *croque monsieur* for lunch, and wash it all down with a French Kiss cocktail. Service is excellent.

Mari Vanna ££££ *93 Zarifa Aliyeva Street; tel: 12-404 9595. Open Mon–Fri noon–midnight, Sat–Sun 10am–midnight.* This is an upmarket Russian restaurant with chandeliers, plush seating and antiques. Try favourites like *borscht,* beef stroganoff or *solyanka.* The service is faultless. Booking essential.

Mirvari ££ *Baku Boulevard, Neftchilar Avenue; tel: 50-247 1515. Open daily 6am–2am.* Meaning 'pearl' in Azeri, this place is legendary in Baku. Its undulating, concrete canopy has been part of the boulevard since 1960, and today, dishes up a menu of delicious and affordable kebabs, salads and hot and cold drinks. Do as the nostalgic Bakuvians do by getting a seat on the raised level to enjoy the sea breeze, all while enjoying a glass of tea and strawberry *mürəbbə*, the local fruit preserve.

Sahil ££££ *34 Neftchilar Avenue; tel: 12-404 8212. Open Sun–Thu noon–midnight, Fri–Sat noon–2am.* Executive chef Simuzar puts her own contemporary spin to traditional food at this hip, upmarket seafront restaurant. There is also an extensive cocktail and spirits menu if you fancy skipping food and just sipping on a tipple in the outdoor seating area.

DOWNTOWN AND FOUNTAINS SQUARE

Cafe Ali and Nino £ *2 Taghiyev Street; tel: 51-312 2440. Open daily 10am–10pm.* This cosy book café hits the spot if you are looking for a quiet coffee or lunch in a busy area. You will find it in the basement of the bookshop of the same name, named after the lovers in Kurban Said's love story about a Muslim Azeri boy and a Christian Georgian girl. The walls are adorned with historical scenes and photos of Bakuvians from the early 20th century.

Cafe Araz ££ *1 Islam Safarli Street; tel: 12-492 4846. Open daily, 24 hours.* The menu at this open-air, wooden terraced café on the edge of Fountains Square entwines Azerbaijani and Turkish cuisines and has some of the most affordable prices in the area. Service may come with a little helping of nonchalant Azeri attitude. A good place to meet friends for a summer lunch.

Dolma Restaurant ££ *8 M. Rasulzada Street; tel: 12-498 1938. Open daily 11am–2am.* This quaint, cellar-esque restaurant is often praised for its value for money and mammoth menu of traditional dishes. To share some starters, try the eponymous *dolma* (stuffed vine leaves) and the *düşbərə* (dumpling stuffed with ground meat). Ask the informed waiters for recommendations.

Firuze £££ *14 Tarlan Aliyarbeyov Street; tel: 12-493 9634. Open daily noon–1am.* On the corner of Fountains Square, this basement restaurant is much loved by locals. Dishes on the 12-page menu here, mostly tra-ditional with a few international options, are both delicious and fairly priced. The ambience is authentic and cosy, with stone walls adorned in traditional rugs and ceramics.

Nargiz Restaurant £££ *9 Tarlan Aliyarbeyov Street; tel: 12-493 9886. Open daily 11am–2am.* The cylindrical Nargiz is bit of an institution in Baku, having been around for more than 30 years. At 70 manat, the *quzu səbət* (lamb, tomato, potato and trimmings) is by far the most expensive thing on the menu, but the hefty lump of grilled lamb is a carnivore's dream and will easily feed 2–3 people.

NASIMI AND YASAMAL

Shirvanshah Museum Restaurant ££ *86 Salatyn Asgarova Street; tel: 50-242 0903. Open daily 9am–midnight.* An unusual, two-storey museum/restaurant hybrid that encapsulates all that is traditionally Azerbaijani. The stone-walled, cobble-floored interior is blanketed in artefacts, from samovars and rugs to copperware and musical instruments. The menu, as expected, is unequivocally Azeri. For a hyper-local dish, try the her-baceous rice dish *səbzi plov*, or *xəngəl*.

THE FLAME TOWERS AND WEST OF THE CITY CENTRE

Darya Fish House ££ *Namiq Quliyev Street; tel: 50-754 4747. Open daily 8am–11.30pm.* This sprawling, Caspian-front restaurant in Bibi-Heybat offers a wide selection of seasonal fish and seafood dishes with sensa-tional sea views. There is an impressive drinks menu, and if you don't know what you want, get the *buğlama* (steamed fish). Stop here for din-ner on your way back from Gobustan.

Nakhchivan ££££ *8A Parliament Avenue; tel: 12-480 8585. Open daily noon–midnight.* This upmarket joint dishes up mouthwatering local dishes from both the region and mainland. Nakhchivan-style speciali-ties include *kyata* (dough stuffed with greens and cheese), *piti* (soup with lamb, potatoes, cherry plum, peas and tomatoes) and *govurma* (lamb or veal stew). There is also a substantial list of spirits. Book ahead.

Telequlle £££ *2 Academic Abbaszadeh Street (TV Tower); tel: 70-770 7070. Open daily 10am–11.45pm.* A revolving restaurant inside the city's iconic 1996 TV tower, the tallest structure in Baku. Panoramic views of the city from here, including the nearby gargantuan Flame Towers, are the main draw, and the menu is a mix of contemporary local and Western dishes. Book ahead. There's a 20 AZN deposit per person.

EAST OF THE CITY CENTRE

Sumakh £££ *20–22 Khojaly Avenue; tel: 12-480 2112. Open daily noon–midnight.* Launched by local restaurant chain The Beat Group, this open-kitchen place has a knack for combining the traditional with the contemporary, both in its menu and decor. Turophiles should try the Azerbaijani Cheese Platter, which comes with a portion of *motal*. Booking advised.

Bəh Bəh Club £££ *67 Nobel Avenue; tel: 50-323 2022. Open daily noon–2am.* This family-style restaurant near Baku White City is mostly unknown to tourists. In Azeri, 'bəh bəh' is an exclamation of joy used to describe anything from delicious food to a great song, both of which come in bounds in this castle-like gem. Chef specialities include *ququ qabırğa dolması* (dolma with lamb rib meat) and the tender-cooked *kütüm lavangi* (fish stuffed with walnuts and onions). The menu is in Azeri and Russian only.

Tonqal £££ *82 Academic Gasan Aliyev Street; tel: 12-449 9198. Open daily 10am–midnight.* Meaning 'bonfire' in Azeri, this antiquarian place, entered via a palatial, metal gate, has its own wine cellar, a beautifully-lit outdoor area and delicious dishes cooked in a traditional tandoor oven. The menu is a hearty mix of local and European food made using locally-sourced ingredients. Staff here are very friendly.

EXCURSIONS

Gala Bazaar ££ *46 Gala Road, tel: 12-559 2999. Open daily, 24 hours.* Stop here on your way to/from the airport or Mardakan. Part restaurant, part bathhouse and part guesthouse, expect all the favourite dishes on its extensive menu, including various *plovs*, *xengel* and *badambura*.

A-Z TRAVEL TIPS

A SUMMARY OF PRACTICAL INFORMATION

A

ACCOMMODATION

The accommodation scene in Baku consists of around 150 hotels, ranging from palatial five-star hotels of international brands like Four Seasons and Fairmont, to smaller, traditional boutique options, with a small number of budget-friendly hostels thrown into the mix. In recent years, as Baku's popularity has risen, more and more hotels have opened up all over the city, and Airbnb and private rental options are slowly on the rise, too, although there aren't too many bed-and-breakfast options.

Prices start from around 50 AZN (£24) per night. With the cheaper options breakfast tends to cost extra. The more expensive rooms often come with Caspian Sea views.

Most reputable hotels are situated in and around the city centre. Booking in advance is essential, especially in summer. A number of hotels offer incentives, such as three nights for the price of one, for booking directly. The busiest months are between April and August, as this is when major sporting events like Formula One and UEFA football games come to town. The majority of hotels stay open year-round, with the cheaper rates, as expected, being in the autumn/winter months.

Pre-planning and booking at least two months in advance is strongly advised thanks to Baku's current tourism boom, but if you do find yourself in need of a room, head to one of the city's tourist offices, or the official tourist board website, www.azerbaijan.travel, which has a travel planning section to help you find somewhere to stay.

Staff at major hotels, especially those in the city centre, speak English, Russian and Turkish. Bookings can be made direct or on major platforms like www.booking.com, as well as on www.bookand.travel and www.swtravel.az.

What's the rate per night? **Bir gecəsi neçəyədir?**

I'd like a single/double room. **Bir/iki nəfərlik yer otaq istəyirəm.**

AIRPORT

Baku's airport, **Heydar Aliyev International Airport (GYD)** (www.air-port.az; tel: 12-497 2727) is situated approximately 25km (15.5 miles) from the city centre. There are three ways to reach the centre of Baku: bus, taxi or personal pick-up. The cheapest is the Aero Express Line bus service, which takes 30 minutes from the airport to the last stop, 28 May Metro Station/Central Railway Station. Buses run daily, every 30 minutes from 6am–7pm, at 7.40pm and 8.10pm, and then every hour between 9pm and 6am. Tickets cost 1.50 AZN or 1.30 AZN for those with a BakuCard city pass, available from the airport.

For taxis, the airport uses the London cab-style Baku White Taxi, which you can order with the help of one of the taxi marshals or at the yellow service point by the exit. The average fare to the city centre is around 25–30 AZN and the journey takes roughly 30 minutes. They accept either cash or card.

How much is it to downtown Baku? **Bakının mərkəzinə neçəyə aparsız?**
Does this bus go to Baku? **Bu avtobus Bakıya gedir?**

 B

BICYCLE HIRE

Cycling is not as popular as in European cities, but for those keen to hire a bicycle, RentaSport Baku (59C Rasul Rza; tel: 51-851 8011; daily 10am–3am) in the city centre offer a good selection of bikes. Hiring a bike for one day costs 20–30 AZN.

BUDGETING FOR YOUR TRIP

Baku is considerably cheaper than London and most cities in Europe, especially when it comes to eating out, and there's a good mix of cheap, mid-range and luxury accommodation options. The most expensive portion of your trip is likely to be the flights.

Accommodation. A double room in a basic hotel in central Baku costs 50–70 AZN per night, in the mid-range category from 70–120 AZN and in the five-star luxury hotels the price tag can go up to 400 AZN and beyond.

Flights. Direct flights from London start from around £567 return, and indirect flights from £170. There is not a huge seasonal difference in flight costs.

Meals and drinks. A meal in Baku can consist of anything from a simple kebab that costs as little as a few manats to a full-blown fine-dining extravaganza that can set you back hundreds. On average, a three-course meal with a soft drink or beer at a mid-range restaurant would cost around 20 AZN, with some offering special lunch menus for 10 AZN or so. A tea can cost anything from 0.50 AZN upwards; a coffee from 2 AZN; local beer 2–4 AZN and a bottle of wine at a local mid-range restaurant starts from around 15 AZN.

Museums. Admission fees range from 1–10 AZN, and some art galleries are free to enter, like QGallery and the Museum of Miniature Books in the Old City.

The handy BakuCard offers free public transport across the city, including discounts for the airport shuttle and half price on the hop-on, hop-off Baku City Tour, free/discounted entry to a selection of museums/attractions and special offers at shops and restaurants. Cards are available online (www.bakucard.az) and at the airport, major hotels, tourism agencies and www.iticket.az website and kiosks. Tickets cost 24 AZN, 45 AZN and 70 AZN for one, three and seven days.

C

CAR HIRE

Driving around the busy streets of Baku can be convoluted, and hiring a car to get around is unnecessary as the city is fairly walkable with a good transport system. If you want to venture to the outskirts on your own however, it's always cheaper to book ahead and online.

Major international brands include **Avis** (tel: 12-497 5455; www.avis.az) and **Europcar** (tel: 51-225 7156; www.europcar.az), and local rental companies include **Karavan** (tel: 55-455 2245; www.karavan.az) and **Aznur** (tel: 50-492 1313; www.aznur.az; daily 24 hours). Aznur is available to book at the airport. A medium-sized car for a weekend costs 98 AZN (online only price) with a 300 AZN deposit.

The minimum age and driving experience for hiring a car depends on the individual company, and ranges from 21–23 years old and 1–2 years' experience. You will need to provide your passport in order to make a booking, and make sure to check the company website regarding insurance and excess costs.

I'd like to rent a car. **Maşın kirayə götürmək istəyirəm.**

CLIMATE

Baku and the Absheron Peninsula experience hot and dry summers, although this is rarely extreme and the breeze from the sea means it's not too stifling. July and August are the hottest months, when temperatures range anywhere from 26°C to 35°C. Winter months are cool with the occasional snow and showers, and temperatures are between 3 and 10°C.

May and June provide ideal sightseeing temperatures of around 23°C. Baku has been nicknamed the 'city of winds' thanks to the year-round winds from the Caspian Sea, and as the lowest-lying capital in the world at 28 metres (92ft) below sea level, there is very little to impede the gusts.

	J	F	M	A	M	J	J	A	S	O	N	D
°C	4	4	7	12	18	23	26	26	16	22	14	7
°F	39	39	45	54	64	73	79	79	61	72	5	45

CLOTHING

During spring and summer, bring light, cool clothing and a jacket for the evening. Overall, Baku sees little precipitation, but it's worth packing an umbrella or a cagoule just in case, especially if you are visiting between October and December when the chance of rainfall is at its highest.

When visiting mosques, women must cover their entire body and wear a headscarf. It's generally wise to avoid wearing revealing clothes when visiting any religious building. Sturdy, comfortable shoes are advised for visiting attractions on the outskirts, where terrain can become uneven.

CRIME AND SAFETY

Generally, crime levels in Baku are very low. However, just like anywhere, it's wise to take sensible precautions, especially at night and around Western bars in the city centre. Avoid carrying large sums of money, walking alone after dark or paying bribes, and always try and use known taxi firms. If you are a victim of any crime, call the police (see Emergencies).

D

DRIVING

Avoid driving on the tricky streets of Baku if you can. Walking is the best way to see the city centre, and for anywhere else, there are sufficient bus, metro and taxi services. Tour operators can also arrange transport for you.

In Azerbaijan driving is on the right, wearing a seatbelt is compulsory and children under the age of 12 must not sit in the front. The speed limit in the city centre is 60km/h (37mph), outside of the centre it's 90km/h (56mph), rising to 120km/h (75mph) on motorways, unless marked otherwise by signs. Azerbaijan has a strict zero drink driving policy, so you must not have a trace of alcohol in your system while behind the wheel. Mobile phone usage is hands-free only.

Road conditions in the centre are generally good, but can become more uneven as you drive into the hinterlands. In case of a breakdown, there is no official service for this, and the best thing to do is call your car rental company.

Are we on the right road? **Biz düz yoldayıq?**
Fill the tank, please. **Benzin doldurun zehmet olmasa.**
My car has broken down. **Maşınım qırılıb.**
There's been an accident. **Qəza baş verib.**

E

ELECTRICITY

Electricity in Azerbaijan is 220/240 with a frequency of 50 Hz. Plug types are C, with two round pins, and F, with two round pins and two earth clips on each side. Visitors from the UK will require an adaptor, but voltage is more or less the same as the UK, so a voltage converter is not necessary.

EMBASSIES AND CONSULATES

For citizens of Canada, Australia, New Zealand, Ireland and South Africa, there are no embassies in Azerbaijan. Citizens of these countries should seek consular assistance from the accredited embassies in Ankara, Turkey, detailed below.

UK 45 Khagani Street, AZ1010; tel: +994 12-437 7878; www.gov.uk/world/azerbaijan

US 111 Azadlig Avenue AZ1007; tel: +994 12-488 3300; https://az.usembassy.gov

Canada Cinnah Caddesi No. 58, Çankaya, 06690; tel: +90 312-409 2700; www.turkey.gc.ca

Australia MNG Building Uğur Mumcu Caddesi No. 88, 7th Floor Gaziosmanpaşa, 06700; tel: +90 312-459 9500; www.turkey.embassy.gov.au

New Zealand Kizkulesi Sokak No.11 Gaziosmanpaşa; tel: +90 312-446 3333; www.mfat.govt.nz

Ireland Ugur Mumcu Caddesi No. 88 MNG Binasi A&B Blok, Kat 1 Gaziosmanpasa, 06700; tel: +90 312-459 1000; www.dfa.ie/turkey

South Africa Filistin Sokak No. 27 Gaziosmanpasa, 06700; tel: +90 312-405 6861; www.southafrica.org.tr

Where is the British embassy? **Britaniya səfirliyi haradadır?**

EMERGENCIES

Fire 101
Police 102
Ambulance 103

English-speaking staff should be available on the phone, but when visiting a police station take someone with you to interpret.

G

GETTING THERE

By air. Air travel is by far the most convenient way of reaching Baku, which is roughly 4,800km (3,000 miles) from the UK. The only direct route from London (Heathrow) to Baku is served by the national carrier **Azerbaijan Airlines** (www.azal.az), which operates three flights per week (four between June and August) and has a flight time of approximately 5.5 hours. A return ticket costs around £567, depending on the date of travel and how empty/full the plane is. The airline also serves the Azeri cities of Ganja, Qabala and Nakhchivan. Airlines offering indirect flights from major UK cities include Turkish Airlines, Ukraine International and Emirates, but beware of long stopovers.

By rail. A railway system connects Baku with other former-Soviet cities including Tbilisi, Moscow and Kiev. Check www.ady.az for further information.

GUIDES AND TOURS

An increasing number of guided private and group tours and excursions operate in and around Baku, and more information on these can be found online, at the airport, tourist offices and major hotels.

Bakusightseeing.com (tel: 12-499 8892; www.bakusightseeing.com) offers an array of tours with multilingual guides, including themed tours, walking tours, hop-on, hop-off bus tours, night walks and excursions to Gobustan and Yanar Dag as well as other destinations in the country.

SalamBaku (tel: 12-498 1244; www.salambaku.travel) is also an excellent hub for general planning and booking tours, theatre tickets and events happening in the city.

Baku Original Walking Free Tour (tel: 50-722 7234; www.bakufreetour.com) offers free daily walking tours in the city, available in English and Azerbaijani. The original tour runs twice daily at 11am and 5pm from Fountains Square (in front of KFC) between April and October, and once a day between November and March. Focussed free tours include the Old Town, Downtown, Night Tour and the Alternative Tour. As usual with free tours, tipping is expected.

We'd like an English-speaking guide. **Biz ingiliscə bilən müşahidəçi istəyirik.**

H

HEALTH AND MEDICAL CARE

Baku is generally a healthy city, although there are still some precautions to take and it's worth checking www.travelhealthpro.org.uk for the latest health advice.

Emergency medical care can be reached around the clock by dialling 103, and it's advised that you obtain good travel insurance which includes serious illness and accident cover before you travel. Note that the reciprocal healthcare agreement between the UK and Azerbaijan ended in 2016.

Avoid drinking water from the tap or water that has not been treated or boiled, and take precautions against possible insect bites. The Azerbaijani word for pharmacy is 'aptek', and those open 24 hours a day, indicated by '24 saat', include Aptek Həyat, Kaspian Aptek and Zəfəran Aptek. There are also Zəfəran Aptek vending machines at the airport. www.aptekonline.az is a handy website for finding the details of your nearest pharmacy.

Major hospitals in Baku include the Central Clinic Hospital (76 Parliament Avenue) and the Bona Dea International Hospital (2 Mehdi Abbasov Street).

Where's the nearest (all night) pharmacy? **Ən yaxın 24 saat aptek haradadır?**
I need a doctor/dentist **Mənə həkim/diş həkimi lazımdır**
an ambulance **təcili yardım**

L

LANGUAGE

Azerbaijani is the national language and belongs to the Turkic language family. There are around 30 million native speakers. In the past, it has used both the Arabic and Cyrllic alphabet, but now uses Latin, and both the language and alphabet is most similar to Turkish. Russian and Turkish are also spoken in Baku, and English is often spoken by the younger generation and staff in major hotels and restaurants. The further out you travel from central Baku, the less likely you are to come across English speakers. Menus in larger restaurants are translated into Russian and English, and many signposts for tourist attractions are in both Azeri and English. It is worth learning a handful of Azerbaijani words and phrases before visiting.

DISTINCTIVE LETTERS

ə is pronounced like the a in 'back', ç is ch, c is j, ğ is a gargled g, q sounds like a hard g, ş is sh, and the undotted ı is somewhat grunted. The letter x sounds like nothing in the English language, and w doesn't exist. The dotted ü sounds like the u in 'mute', and ö is like the 'er' in 'her'.

LGBTQ TRAVELLERS

Even though homosexuality has been legal in Azerbaijan since 2000, LGBTQ individuals keep a low profile and extremely few openly declare their orientation due to conservative views and little social acceptance. The gay scene in Baku is pretty much non-existent, and public displays of affection are best avoided.

M

MAPS

Free tourist and transport maps can be obtained at the airport, hotels and tourist information offices. Some maps focus on tourist areas like the Old City as well as wider Baku. Maps of Baku Metro can also be downloaded on www.metro.gov.az. Useful regional map websites include www.gomap.az and www.bakumaps.com, which helps to pinpoint hotels, museums, restaurants, travel agencies and car rentals across the city.

MEDIA

Newspapers. The weekly *AzerNews* (www.azernews.az) was founded in 1997 and is published in English, covering a range of issues across Azerbaijan, including politics, business, sports and entertainment. It's available both online and in print; it can be pick up from any of the city's kiosks. Major daily newspapers printed in Azerbaijani include *Azərbaycan, Xalq Gəzeti, Adalat, Respublika* and *525-ci Qəzet*. A handful of newspapers are printed in Russian, like the daily *Bakinskiy Rabochiy*.

Radio. Major radio stations include 106 FM, Day.az, Azad Azərbaycan and ASAN Radio. The latter two broadcast weekly segments in English.

Television. The four main television stations in Azerbaijan are AzTV, İdman Azərbaycan, Mədəniyyət TV and İTV. The latter became a member of the European Broadcasting Union in 2007, allowing Azerbaijan to compete in the Eurovision Song Contest. Larger hotels tend to offer English-speaking channels including BBC, Sky News and CNN.

MONEY

Currency. The official currency in Azerbaijan is the manat (AZN, ₼), which is divided into 100 qəpik (coins). Manat notes come in denominations of 1, 5, 10, 20, 100 and 200, and coins come in denominations of 1, 3, 5 10, 20 and 50.

Exchange facilities. Major currencies including dollars, pounds and euros can easily be exchanged at banks, exchange offices and booths dotted around Baku. Exchange rates at facilities vary only slightly, banks are probably your best bet for a slightly better rate. Make sure to change your manats back to your home currency before returning as this is impossible to do outside Azerbaijan.

Credit cards and cash machines. Most hotels, larger restaurants and shops accept Mastercard/Visa. In hyper-local restaurants and bazaars, you will need to pay with cash. You can withdraw manat from one of the many ATMs available in Baku. It's worth checking how much your bank charges for foreign withdrawals before travelling.

Can I pay with a credit card? **Kredit kartı ilə ödəyə bilərəm?**
I want to change some dollar/pounds. **Bir az dollar/ sterlinq dəyişdirmək istəyirəm.**
How much is this? **Bu neçəyədir?**
Where's the nearest bank/currency exchange office? **Ən yaxın bank/pul dəyişmə məntəqəsi haradadır?**

O

OPENING TIMES

Typically, banks are open Mon–Fri 10am–5pm. Most shops and super-markets are open daily and close between 9 and 11pm. Bars and restaurants stay open later, especially at weekends. Museums are usually closed on Mondays. Mosques are usually open during normal business hours, but check each one before visiting. Daily bazaars like Taza Bazar and Yashil Bazar are open from around 6–8am until 7–10pm. Bars and restaurants remain open during Ramadan.

P

POLICE (See Also Emergencies)

There's a reassuring amount of police presence on the streets of Baku, and policemen can be identified by their dark blue uniforms and hats bearing the emblem of Azerbaijan. The Main Police Department of

Baku City (tel: 12-493 7987; www.bakupolice.gov.az) is located on 45 Yusif Safarov Street. If you need to call the police, dial 102.

> Where is the nearest police station? **Ən yaxın polis məntəqəsi haradadır?**
> I've lost my wallet/bag/passport. **Mən pul gabimi/çantamı/ pasportumu itirmişəm.**

POST OFFICE

The Azerbaijani postal service is run by Azərpoçt (www.azerpost.az). Post offices in Baku are, as a general rule, open during normal business hours. The main post office is located on 72 Uzeyir Hajibeyov Street, just by Government House, and is open Mon–Sat 9am–7pm, Sun 9am–6pm. Post boxes are green.

> Where is the nearest post office? **Ən yaxın poçt şöbəsi haradadır?**

PUBLIC/NATIONAL HOLIDAYS

Public holidays, including Novruz, Republic Day and Azerbaijan Armed Forces Day, are non-working days, although some businesses stay open. National holidays, including Independence Day, are classed as working days. Restaurants and bars stay open during religious holidays.

1–2 January *Yeni il* New Year
20 January *Qara Yanvar* Black January
8 March *Qadınlar günü* International Women's Day
20–24 March *Novruz Bayrami* Novruz Holiday
31 March *Mart Hadisələri* March Days (Genocide Day)
9 May *Qələbə Günü* Victory Day

28 May *Respublika Günü* Republic Day
15 June *Azərbaycan Xalqının Milli Qurtuluş Günü* National Salvation Day
26 June *Azərbaycan Silahlı Qüvvələri Günü* Day of Armed Forces
18 October *Azərbaycanın Müstəqillik Günü* Independence Day
9 November *Dövlet Bayragi Günü* Flag Day
12 November *Azərbaycan konstitusiyası Günü* Constitution Day
31 December *Dünya Azerbaycanlıların Hemreylik Günü* International Solidarity Day of Azerbaijanis
Moveable dates:
Ramazan Ramadan
Gurban Bayram Festival of Sacrifice

R

RELIGION

Azerbaijan is a secular state, while the majority of the population follows Islam (Shia). Religiously, it's very tolerant; women are not expected to cover their hair (and very few do) and alcohol is served in all bars and restaurants, even during Ramadan. When entering a mosque, women are expected to cover their body and hair (see Clothing).

T

TELEPHONES

The international dialling code for Azerbaijan is 994. The local area code for Baku is 12 and for mobile phones it's 50. To call Azerbaijan from abroad, dial 00994 plus the local number. To make an international call from Azerbaijan, use the international dialling code, followed by the area code and number. Public payphones are sparse.

Mobile phones. Azerbaijan is outside of the EU, so it's best to check roaming charges with your phone operator before travelling as these can be quite high. 3G services are available in metro stations as well as in tunnels. The three phone networks in Azerbaijan are Azercell, Bakcell and Nar.

If you plan on staying for a while or using your mobile phone a lot, it's advised to pick up a local pre-paid SIM-card, available from the airport or from any of the main network shops which you can find dotted around Fountains Square. To use your local SIM-card for more than 30 days, you must register it at the phone shop, post office or online. To do this, you will need a passport and a certificate permitting you to remain in Azerbaijan for more than 30 days.

TIME ZONES

Azerbaijan Standard Time is three hours ahead of Greenwich Mean Time (GMT+3). In 2016, Azerbaijan scrapped daylight saving time. When it's noon in Baku, it's 9am in London, 4am in New York, 10am in Johannesburg, 6pm in Sydney and 8pm in Auckland.

What is the time? **Saat neçədir?**

TIPPING

Tipping is not expected, but is commonplace in Baku. Service charge in most restaurants is 5–10 percent of the total bill. If there is no service charge included, you can tip 10 percent. The normal tipping amount for guides, airport and hotel staff is 5 AZN. For taxis with meters, it's normal to round up the cost. It's not expected to tip in bars.

TOILETS

Public toilets are few and far between in Baku, and most of them are squat toilets. There are a few located underground along the boulevard and in public areas, and there's usually an entrance fee of around 30 qəpik, which you pay to the attendant. If you ask politely, restaurants and bars should allow you to use their facilities. Shopping centres also offer free toilets.

> Where are the toilets? **Tualetlər haradadır?**

TOURIST INFORMATION

The National Tourism Promotion Bureau (www.ntpb.az) heads up the official tourist board Azerbaijan Tourism Board (www.azerbaijan.travel) and the Baku-focussed #SalamBaku (www.salambaku.travel). The main tourist information point (also #SalamBaku) is the Baku Tourism Information Centre at 70 Uzeyir Hajibeyov Street (tel: 12-498 1244; Mon–Fri 9am–6pm, Sat–Sun 11am–4pm). The centre has a helpful team and offers help with tours, maps, transport timetables and free general information about the city. You can also purchase the Baku-Card here to save money on attractions, shops and restaurants. There are also little information booths dotted around the main tourist areas of the city.

TRANSPORT

Metro. Baku's efficient and affordable metro system (tel: 12-490 0000; www.metro.gov.az) operates three lines; red, green and purple, with most of the tourist-centric stops, like the Old City, situated on the red line. It serves 25 stations and currently there is no metro service available at the airport. Trains run from 6am until midnight and the frequency is around every two to three minutes.

To use the metro you need to purchase and load up a pre-paid metro card called BakıKART (www.bakikart.az), available from metro stations, bus stops and the airport. These are scanned at the turnstiles, like in most large cities. There are two types of card; plastic for locals and regular users (2 AZN), and paper for visitors (0.20 AZN). One, two, three or four passes can be loaded onto the paper card, which is valid for 45 days and cannot be topped up. Plastic cards can be topped up using 10, 20, 50 coins, and 1, 5, 10, 20, 50 and 100 notes, but not debit or credit cards. A single fare costs 30 qəpik regardless of distance.

The metro in Baku is generally safe, and some trains are considerably older than others. Be aware that guards may ask to see the contents of your bag for security reasons and you are not permitted to take photographs in metro stations. Works are currently being undertaken to extend the metro network to 76 stations by 2030.

Bus. Buses in Baku are numbered and are another inexpensive way of travelling around the city. A single ride costs 20 qəpik, and on most fleets you pay the driver directly, however the newer red buses (www.bakubus.az) only accept the pre-paid BakıKART. The red bus route has an extensive list of stops and major bus stations including Azneft Square (for Bulvar and Old City), MUM (for Nizami Street and Fountains Square) and the central 28 May station.

Bus routes are available from www.gomap.az. The international bus terminal is called Avtovağzal (www.avtovagzal.az), which runs buses to destinations all over Azerbaijan and international cities including Moscow, Tbilisi and Istanbul. The tram system in Baku was dismantled in 2004, but there are currently talks about restoring it along the boulevard as part of the city's Baku White City development project.

Where can I get a taxi? **Taksi haradan tapa bilərəm?**
Where is the nearest bus stop? **Ən yaxın avtobus dayanacağı haradadır?**
I want a ticket to... **bilet istəyirəm**
single/return **gediş/gediş gəliş**
Will you tell me when to get off? **Mənə deyəbilərsinizmi nə vaxt düşməliyəm?**

Trains. Trains are operated by Azerbaijan Railways (tel: 12-499 4515; www.ady.az). The main railway station in Baku is Baku Central Railway Station on Khatai Avenue, which connects Baku with cities across Azerbaijan as well as cities in Russia, Georgia, Turkey and Ukraine. Routes, schedules, fares and online ticket purchasing are available on the Azerbaijan Railways website.

Taxis. The most reliable taxis are the purple, London cab-style taxis (www.bakitaksi.az), which are fitted with meters and available at the airport and all over the streets of Baku. They are nicknamed 'badımcan' by locals, which means aubergine in Azerbaijani, thanks to their resemblance to the vegetable. Check that the meter is working before you set off.

A trip from the airport (where the London-style cabs are white) to the city centre should cost you around 20 AZN, and around the centre, anywhere between 4 and 15 AZN, depending on distance and time of day. The tariffs start at 0.7 AZN per one kilometre (0.6 mile). They are fairly easy to hail and can also be ordered by calling 1848. A useful taxi ordering service is 189 Taxi (tel: 12-4370 189; www.189taxi.az), available as an app. Uber is also available. Older taxis, especially the boxy Soviet-era Ladas, are more common on the outskirts these days. If you do use an unmetered taxi, it's very important to agree the price before travel to avoid any shocks, especially if you are a foreigner.

Funicular. Baku's funicular runs from Shovkat Alakbarova Street just off Neftchilar Avenue to the city's highest point, Highland Park/Alley of Martyrs. The full journey takes 7–10 minutes and the frequency is around every 20 minutes. A one-way ticket costs 1 AZN. It's open Tue–Sun 10am–1pm and has two stations, Bahram Gur and Alley of Martyrs. The funicular first opened in 1960 and has been renovated several times, most recently in 2012.

TRAVELLERS WITH DISABILITIES

Baku isn't the easiest city for getting around in a wheelchair, especially on public transport or through the cobbled streets of the Old City. Apart from the two newer stations of Avtovağzal (Bus Terminal) and Memar Əcəmi, both on the new Purple Line, access in and out of the metro is stairs/escalator only. Bus ramps are only available on the new red fleet, but these do not cover the whole city. Major museums like Azerbaijan Carpet Museum and Heydar Aliyev Cultural Center are wheelchair friendly.

V

VISAS AND ENTRY REQUIREMENTS

Citizens of the UK require a visa to enter Azerbaijan. An online visa system (www.evisa.gov.az), introduced in 2017, issues visas within three days. Visas cost £19 ($23) including service fee. Once approved, you will receive your visa via email, and must bring a copy of it with you when you travel.

An electronic visa is valid for 30 days and is single entry. You must have six months validity on your passport. If you are staying for longer than 15 days, you must register with the State Migration Service within 15 days. To register, and for the rules and terms of extending your visa visit www.migration.gov.az (202 Binagadi Highway, 3123 Block; tel: 12-565 6118). It's also possible to apply for a visa using the Azerbaijan Embassy-affiliated Visa Service Centre (www.visaforazerbaijan.org.uk) in the UK.

Citizens of US, Canada, Australia, New Zealand, Ireland and South Africa also require a visa.

W

WEBSITES AND INTERNET ACCESS

www.salambaku.travel Official tourist website for Baku
www.azerbaijan.travel Official tourist website for Azerbaijan
www.azal.az The national airline
www.airport.az Heydar Aliyev International Airport
www.bakucard.az The official sightseeing card
www.citylife.az A database of restaurants, theatres and shopping
www.azernews.az English newspaper covering a variety of topics in Azerbaijan

www.bakuexplorer.com Tourist information website
www.gomap.az Interactive map with public transport routes
Free Wi-Fi is available in most hotels, bars, cafés, restaurants and museums, as well as in a handful of parks and outdoor tourist areas. The metro system connects to 3G.

RECOMMENDED HOTELS

Baku has stepped up its accommodation game over the last decade, with a mixed bag of options including five-star hotels with all the trimmings, small traditional boutique hotels, spacious private apartments and the odd backpacker-friendly hostel. Airbnbs are in short supply, although slowly increasing. The list below is divided geographically, with the Old City and the areas surrounding Fountains Square and Neftchilar Avenue the most popular among tourists.

During Formula 1 and UEFA games, prices can increase significantly. Booking direct and at least three months ahead of time via the hotel's official website is almost always the best option, as they often run discount deals, for example three nights for the price of one. A few of them have a minimum night policy.

For those seeking somewhere central with lots of character, the many boutique hotels in the Old City are ideal and affordable by European standards. Most have balconies and are housed in stone-clad, historic buildings, but this means they often lack a lift. Hotels away from the centre are few and far in between, apart from the beach resorts.

The following ranges give an idea of the price for a double room, including VAT and service. Breakfast tends to be included unless stated otherwise, and most hotels accept credit cards.

££££	over £100
£££	£60–100
££	£30–60
£	under £30

ICHERI SHEHER (OLD CITY)

Altstadt Hotel £ *3/2 A Ilyas Efendiyev Street; tel: 12-492 6402.* The eight rooms at this two-star hotel are very simple but the price, especially considering the location, is the cheapest in town. The buffet breakfast is served in what resembles an Azeri aunt's living room, with a piano and a mishmash of traditional decorations. The tea is poured out of a colourful samovar. Backgammon boards are available for anyone who wishes to play.

Buta Hotel ££ *16 Gasser Street; tel: 12-492 3475; www.butahotel.com.* Tucked in one of the Old City's many labyrinthine alleyways, this three-star guesthouse offers homely rooms that are clean and comfortable. The intimate lobby is decorated with samovars, copperware and tradi-tional rugs, with a reception that is open 24 hours a day. Breakfast is served in the small yet bright fourth-floor restaurant, with city views.

Old City Inn ££ *10 Kichik Gala Street, tel: 12-497 4369.* This stone-clad inn is ideally located on one of the Old City's main streets. There are 15 en-suite bedrooms spread across four floors, (if you want a room with a fantastic view, ask for room seven). There is also an onsite restaurant. Beware: this hotel is sometimes used to train hospitality students so things might not always be smooth-sailing.

Museum Inn Boutique Hotel £££ *3 Gazi Mahammad Street; tel: 12-497 1522; www.museuminn.az.* The main draws of this hyper-central, stone-clad hotel is the top-floor restaurant/terrace where you can dine with a summer breeze and a beautiful view of the Maiden Tower and the Cas-pian Sea. The large yet cosy, rug-clad rooms are a good mix of old and new, with all the amenities you would expect at a four-star hotel.

Seven Rooms Boutique Hotel ££ *27 Boyuk Gala Street; tel: 12-505 5901; www.sevenrooms.az.* As the name suggests, there are only seven rooms in this clean and modern boutique hotel, just yards away from major sights like the Maiden Tower and Shirvanshah's Palace. There is no breakfast or restaurant services here but there are plenty of cafés nearby. Rooms are available with balconies and city views, and the staff downstairs are happy to help with everything from restaurant recom-mendations to booking guided tours.

Shah Palace Hotel £££ *47 Qosha Qala Street; tel: 12-497 0405; www. shahpalacehotel.com.* This place is a bit like stepping into an opulent Aladdin's cave. The main draw at this 19th-century former residential building is the four-storey courtyard, decked out with regal velvet sofas, marble ogee arches and chestnut-coloured wooden balconies. Breakfast is served on the fourth-floor terrace at Xanadan restaurant, and there is also a small gym and a beautifully-tiled hammam.

Sultan Inn £££ *20 Boyuk Gala Street; tel: 12-437 2305-10;* www.sultaninn. com. This 11-roomed (four superior, seven standard) boutique hotel is unbeatable for location, with the city's beloved Maiden Tower just yards away. Rooms are a good blend of trendy and comfortable, with some offering sea views. The Terrace Garden restaurant on the roof overlooks the boulevard and Old City, and serves up delicious Azeri dishes like *düşbara, plov* and *qutab.* There is an impressive menu of local and international wines, too.

Two Seasons Boutique Hotel £££ *5 Sabir Street; tel: 55-207 8090.* Light, airy and spacious, this pastel-hued hotel is an absolute gem right in the heart of the Old City. There are just six minimalist-chic rooms, some of which come with huge, city- and sea-facing balconies. The terrace at the front, complete with a white-picket fence, is perfect for a traditional, alfresco Azeri breakfast and is rated highly among guests. The staff are friendly and efficient, and they will even pick you up from the airport for free.

BOULEVARD AND NEFTCHILAR AVENUE

Art Gallery Hotel ££££ *105 Neftchilar Avenue; tel: 12-504 0057;* www.art galleryhotel.az. This super chic, seafront boutique hotel shares its vicinity with the likes of Dior and BVLGARI and is within easy reach of both the Old City and Fountains Square. Playing true to its name, the inside is adorned with loud and abstract works of art by the likes of Brazilian artist Romero Britto and legendary local landscape painter Sattar Bahlulzade. Decor aside, the staff are attentive, the rooms are spacious and the bathrooms are stocked with Hermes products.

Four Seasons Hotel Baku ££££ *1 Neftchilar Avenue; tel: 12-404 2424;* www.fourseasons.com/baku. The crème de la crème of hotels. The opulent, Beaux-Arts-inspired Four Seasons sits on the affluent Neftchilar Avenue, with its own private driveway, 171 rooms and suites that come with either sea or city views. Its emerald-green rooftop has become somewhat iconic, and the lobby is decked out with a grand, Hollywood-esque staircase, marble floors and blinding chandeliers. This is often where celebrities or foreign politicians stay if they are in Baku.

SAHIL Hostel & Hotel £ *27 Zarifa Aliyeva Street; tel: 50-888 2101;* www.sahilhostel.com. This gem is ideal for those with a small budget but big on location. The colourful hostel is conveniently located just 100metres/yds away from the boulevard. It's clean, friendly, and has an on-site bar with local drinks. Dorm rooms are available for up to 10 people, and there are also private rooms with en-suite bathrooms and balconies. Great value for those who would rather spend their money on restaurants and sightseeing.

DOWNTOWN AND FOUNTAINS SQUARE

Azcot Hotel ££ *7 Azerbaijan Avenue, Lane 1; tel: 12-497 2507;* www.azcothotel.com. Right opposite the buzzy Fountains Square, this 1885 former stone mansion was built during the oil boom of Baku and is now home to 38 basic but functional hotel rooms. The hotel caters more towards British guests (thanks to the BP employees who worked in Baku), from the hot, full English breakfast to the more surprising three-pin electrical sockets. There is also a comfortable communal space, rooms with square-facing balconies and photos dotted around depicting the building's wealthy beginnings.

Baku Palace Hotel ££ *23 Islam Safarli Street; tel: 12-497 6271;* www.bakupalacehotel.com. A stay at this unassuming guesthouse is a bit like staying at a wealthy Azeri family house. It sits a few streets north of Fountains Square, just creeping into the south of Yasamal raion. Inside, expect a living room area with a chandelier and a grand piano, tons of parquet flooring and comfortable, silky bedding. All rooms come with a balcony and a private bathroom. For the price, it's an excellent choice, especially for those on a budget who want to avoid faceless hotels.

Passage Hotel ££ *53B Nizami Street; tel: 55-404 0051;* www.passagehotel.az. The history of this building dates back a century and a few of its 12 rooms still bear the original stone walls. Its location on one of Baku's main roads is unbeatable, with a plethora of shops, restaurants and bars right on the doorstep. Rooms are comfortable, and those with balconies are worth the extra cost. Like most of the older buildings in the city, there is no lift. The food will not blow you away, but you are spoilt for choice with restaurants close by. Beware: the staff may not speak perfect English.

Prestige Hotel £££ *5 Mirza Ibrhahimov Street; tel: 12-595 1663*. This place is plush yet homely. Housed inside a historic, whitewashed stone building, moments from the bustling Fountains Square and Nizami Street, it's decked out with extra-large beds and gold decor. It offers all the necessities you would need, including fast Wi-Fi, soundproof rooms (the area can get a little noisy) and room service. The breakfast is rated very highly here, and so are the staff, who know the city inside out.

Salam Baku Hotel ££ *1 Khagani Street; tel: 12-493 3100; www.salambaku hotel.az*. The pillar-fronted hotel is in the perfect location, right by Molo-kan Garden and overlooking the chandelier-lined Nizami Street. Rooms are spacious and a continental breakfast is included. There are also tons of cafés and restaurants moments from here.

Theatrum Hotel Baku £££ *Mardanov Brothers; tel: 12-525 5525; www.c-group.az*. The new, colourful Roman-style hotel is often commended for the friendliness and efficiency of its staff. It comes with a verdant ter-race, spacious rooms and Tavada restaurant which serves up a mix of local and European dishes. There are also regular music gigs. Bear in mind that the budget double room does not have a window.

THE FLAME TOWERS AND WEST OF THE CITY CENTRE

Crescent Beach Hotel £££ *Salyan Highway; tel: 12-497 4777; www.cbh.az*. Take the four-star rating here with a pinch of salt. The decor is a little dated (it's Baku's first ever beach resort) and service is a little slow, but if you want the beach right at your doorstep, then this is not a bad option. The 260-room resort, particularly popular with business travellers, is around 12km (7 miles) south of the boulevard (so not ideal if you want to explore the city on foot), and comes with a fairly large private beach.

Fairmont Baku Flame Towers ££££ *Flame Towers, 1A Mehdi Huseyn Street; tel: 12-565 4848;* www.fairmont.com/baku. Housed inside one of Azerbaijan's modern architectural marvels, this mammoth, five-star hotel boasts 318 luxurious rooms and 19 serviced apartments. The location is both a blessing and a curse; it's within a 20-minute walk of the city's main attractions but sits on top of a hill surrounded by roads that are not always easy to cross. Much like its exterior, everything feels very grand; the lobby's high ceilings, the giant pillars and the 20ft, custom-made chandelier in the shape of a droplet of water. There are a whopping 36 floors in total with floor-to-ceiling windows, so acrophobes should avoid the higher floors.

EAST OF THE CITY CENTRE

Terrace Hotel ££ *10B Babek Avenue; tel: 12-480 1406;* www.terrace.az. Located on the 19th floor of a residential block, this 10-roomed boutique hotel is just a little outside of the city centre. As the name suggests, its terrace is the main lure, with panoramic views of Baku and the prominent Heydar Aliyev Center. The nearest metro station, Khatai, is a 10-minute walk away.

EXCURSIONS

Bilgah Beach Hotel ££££ *94 Gelebe Street; tel: 12-565 4000;* www.bilgah beachhotel.com. This uber-luxurious five-star (formerly Jumeirah) resort is ideal for making the most of one of Baku's best beaches. On top of 176 sea-facing rooms and three-bedroom cottages with their own terrace and car park, there is also a private beach, a fantastic spa and even a basketball court. This place is royally fancy.

DICTIONARY

ENGLISH–AZERBAIJANI

adj adjective   **adv** adverb   **BE** British English   **n** noun   **prep** preposition   **v** verb

A

accept v qabul etmak
access n buraxılış
accident hadisa
accommodation cihaz
account n (**bank**) hesab (bank hesabı)
acupuncture aku-punktura
adapter adapter
address n ünvan
admission (price) giriş qiymati (qiymat)
after sonra; ~**noon** günorta; ~**shave** taraş
age n yaş
agency agentlik
AIDS QİCS
air n hava; ~ **conditioning** havanın kondisiyalaşdırılması; ~ **dry** quru havalı; ~ **pump** hava pompası; ~**line** avia xatt; ~**mail** aviapoçt; ~**plane** tayyara; ~**port** hava limanı
aisle keçid; ~ **seat** keçiddə yer
allergic allergik; ~ **reaction** allergik reaksiya
allow icaza vermak
alone tak (tanhalıqda)
alter v dayişmak

alternate route alternativ yol
aluminum foil alüminium folqası
amazing möcüzali
ambulance tacili yardım
American adj amerikanlı
amusement park aylanca parkı
anemic azqanlı
anesthesia anesteziya
animal heyvan
ankle topuq
antibiotic n antibiotik
antiques store suvenir mağazası
antiseptic cream antiseptik krem
apartment manzil
appendix (body part) appendiks (badanin hissasi)
appetizer qalyanaltı
appointment tayinat
arcade arkada
area code vilayatin kodu
arm n (**body part**) qol (badanin hissasi)
aromatherapy aromat-erapiya
around (the corner) yaxında (küncün arxasında); ~ (**price**) taxmini qiymat
arrival galma

arrive galmak
artery arteriya
arthritis artrit
art icasanat
Asian adj asiyalı
aspirin aspirin
asthmatic astmatik
ATM bankomat; ~ **card** bankomat üçün kart
attack v hücum etmak
attraction (place) calb etma (yer üzra)
attractive calbedici
Australia Avstraliya
Australian adj avstraliyalı
automatic avtomatik; ~ **car** avtomatik maşın
available alçatan

B

baby uşaq; ~ **bottle** uşaq butulkası; ~ **wipe** uşaq salfetlari; ~**sitter** daya
back (body part) kürak (badanin hissasi); ~**ache** kürakda ağrı; ~**pack** çanta
bag çanta
baggage [BE] baqaj; ~ **claim** baqajın verilmasi; ~ **ticket** baqaj qabzi
bake v tormoz

bakery çörak dükanı
ballet balet
bandage sarğı
bank n bank
bar (place) bar (yer)
barbecue (device) n barbekü (qurğu barbekü üçün qril)
barber barbar
baseball beysbol
basket (grocery store) sabat (arzaq dükanında)
basketball basketbol
bathroom vanna otağı
battery batareya
battleground döyüş meydanı
be v olmaq
beach çimarlik
beautiful gözal
bed n çarpayı; ~ **and breakfast** çarpayı va sahar yemayi
before avval
begin başlamaq
beginner başlayan
behind (direction) arxada (istiqamat)
beige adj bej
belt qayış
best adj an yaxşısı; ~ **before** yaxşısı qabaq istifada etmak
better daha yaxşı
bicycle velosiped

big böyük; ~ger artıq
bike route velosiped yolu
bikini bikini
bill n (money) hesab (pul); ~ n (of sale) qabz
bird quş
birthday ad günü
black adj qara
bladder sidik kisəsi
bland yüngül
blanket yorğan
bleed qan axmaq
blender blender
blood qan; ~ pressure qan təzyiqi
blouse köynək
blue adj göy
board v bort; ~ing pass minmə talonu
boat n qayıq
boil v qaynadmaq
bone n sümük
book n kitab; ~store kitab mağazası
boot n çəkmə
boring darıxdırıcı
botanical garden botanik bağ
bother v narahat olmaq
bottle n butulka; ~ opener butulkanı açmaq üçün quğu
bowl n kasa
boxing match boks matçı
boy oğlan; ~friend dost
bra lifçik
bracelet qolbaq
brake (car) tormoz (maşında)
breaded unlanmış
break v (bone) sındırmaq (sümüyü)

breakdown (car) baxış (maşının)
breakfast n səhər yeməyi
break in (burglary) n qırma (soymaq məqsədi ilə)
breast döş; ~feed v əmizdirmak
breathe nəfəs almaq
bridge körpü
briefs (clothing) alt tumanı (geyim)
bring gətirmək
British adj britaniyalı
broken sınmış ~ (bone) sınmış sümük
brooch sancaq
broom süpürgə
brother qardaş
brown adj qəhvəyi
bug (insect) n böcək (həşərat)
building bina
burn v yandırmaq
bus n avtobus; ~ station avtobus stansiyası; ~ stop avtobus dayanacağı; ~ ticket avtobusda gediş üçün bilet; ~ tour avtobusda tur
business adj biznes; ~ card biznes kartı; ~ center biznes mərkəzi; ~ class biznes sinif ; ~ hours iş saatları
butcher n qəssab
buttocks yan
buy v almaq
bye hələlik

C

cabaret kabare
cable car funikulyor

cafe (place) kafe (yer)
call v (phone) zəng vurmaq (telefonla); ~ n çağırmaq ~ collect abunəçinin hesabına zəng vurmaq
calorie kaloriya
camera kamera; ~ case kameranın çexolu; digital ~ rəqəmli kamera
camp v düşərgə; ~ing stove yürüş sobası; ~site düşərgənin yerləşməsi
can opener konserv bankalarının açılması üçün qurğu
Canada Kanada
Canadian adj kanadalı
cancel ləğv
candy konfet
canned good konservləşdirilmiş məhsul
canyon kanyon
car maşın; ~ hire [BE] maşını sifariş etmək; ~ park [BE] maşını saxlamaq; ~ rental maşını icarəyə götürmək; ~ seat maşında oturacaq
carafe qrafin
card n kart; ATM ~ bankomat kartı; credit ~ kredit kartı; debit ~ debet kartı; phone ~ telefon kartı
carry on n (piece of hand luggage) əl yükü (əl baqajı)
cart (grocery store) araba (ərzaq dükanından); ~ (luggage) baqaj arabası

carton (of cigarettes) siqaret paçkası ; ~ (of groceries) ərzaqlar üçün karton paketi
cash n pul; ~ v ödəmək
cashier kassadar
casino kazino
castle qıfıl
cathedral kilsə
cave n mağara
CD SD diski
cell phone mobil telefonu
Celsius Selsi dərəcəsi
centimeter santimetr
certificate sertifikat
chair n oturacaq; ~ lift asma qaldırıcısı
change v (baby) dəyişmək (uşaq bezi); ~ (buses) avtobusa minmək; ~ (money) pulları dəyişmək; ~ n (money) sdəç (pul)
charge v (credit card) ödəniş (kredit kartdan); ~ (cost) ödənişin dəyəri
cheap ucuz; ~er daha ucuz
check v (luggage) baqaj qəbzi; ~ (on something) nə isə yoxlamaq; ~ (payment) qəbz (ödəniş üzrə); ~ in yoxlamaq; ~ing account hesabı yoxlamaq; ~ out ... baxmaq
Cheers! ! Sağlam olasız
chemical toilet biotualet
chemist [BE] kimyəvi
chest (body part) sinə (bananın hissəsi); ~ pain sinədə ağrı

chewing gum saqqız
child ; **~'s seat** uşaq kreslosu
children's menu uşaq menyüsü
children's portion uşaq porsiyası
Chinese adj çin
chopsticks yemak üçün çöplar
church kilsa
cigar siqara
class n sinif; **business ~** biznes sinifi; **economy ~** ekonom sinif; **first ~** birinci sinif
classical music klassik musiqi
clean v tamizlamak; **~** adj **(clothes)** tamiz (geyim); **~ing product** tamizlamak üçün mahsul
clear v **(on an ATM)** silmak (bankomatda daxil etmak üçün satır)
cliff sıldırım qaya
cling film [BE] yapışqan qaysaq
close v **(a shop)** bağlamaq (mağaza)
closed bağlıdır
clothing geyim; **~ store** geyim mağazası
club n klub
coat örtük
coin sikka
colander süzgac
cold n **(sickness)** soyuqdayma (xastalik); **~** adj **(temperature)** soyuq (temperatur)
colleague hamkar

cologne odekolon
color n rang
comb n daraq
come v galmak
complaint şikayat
computer kompüter
concert konsert; **~ hall** konsert zalı
condition (medical) vaziyyat (sahhatin)
conditioner (hair) saçlara qulluq üçün vasita
condom prezervativ
conference konfrans
confirm tasdiq etmak
congestion (medical) durğunluq (orqanizmda)
connect (internet) birlaşmak (internet)
connection (travel/internet) (/) alaqa (sayahatlar/internet); **~ flight** birlaşma reysi
constipated çirklanmiş
consulate konsulluq
consultant maslahatçi
contact v alaqaya girmak
contact lens kontakt linzaları; **~ solution** kontakt linzalar üçün mahlul
contagious yoluxucu
convention hall iclas zalı
conveyor belt konveyer xatti
cook v hazırlamaq
cool adj **(temperature)** sarin (temperatur)
copper n mis
corkscrew n burğu

cost v xarclar
cotton pambıq
cough v öskürmak; **~** n öskürak
country code ölkanin kodu
cover charge alava dayar
cream (ointment) krem (maz)
credit card kredit kartı
crew neck yumru kasik
crib uşaq çarpayısı
crystal n **(glass)** büllur (şüşa)
cup n fincan
currency valyuta; **~ exchange** valyuta mübadilasi; **~ exchange office** valyuta mübadila mantaqasi
current account [BE] cari hesab
customs gömrük nazarati
cut v kasmak; **~** n **(injury)** kasik (yara)
cute aziz
cycling velosipedda getma

D

damage v zadalamak
dance v raqs etmak; **~ club** raqs klubu; **~ing** raqs edan
dangerous tahlükali
dark adj tünd
date n **(calendar)** tarix (taqvim)
day gün
deaf adj kar
debit card debet kartı
deck chair şezlonq

declare v **(customs)** gömrükda aşyaları taqdim etmak
decline v **(credit card)** qabul etmamak (kredit kartını)
deep adj darin
degree (temperature) daraca (temperatur)
delay v gecikdirmak
delete v **(computer)** aradan qaldırmaq (kompüter)
delicatessen qastronomiya mağazası
delicious dadlı
denim pambıq parça
dentist dantist
denture diş protezlaması
deodorant dezodorant
department store univermaq
departure (plane) uçuş (tayyara)
deposit v **(money)** qoymaq (pulları); **~** n **(bank)** banka amanat
desert n sahra
detergent tamizlayan vasita
develop v **(film)** fotoplyonkanı etmak
diabetic adj diabetik; n diabetik
dial v nömrani yığmaq
diamond almaz
diaper uşaq bezi
diarrhea ishal
diesel dizel yanacağı
difficult mürakkab
digital raqamli; **~ camera** raqamli kamera; **~ photo** raqamli fotoşakil; **~ print** raqamli çap

dining room yeməkxana

dinner nahar

direction istiqamət

dirty çirkin

disabled adj **(person)** işləmək qabiliyyətini itirmiş (əlil); **~ accessible** [BE] əlillərə əlçatan

disconnect (computer) ayırmaq (kompüteri)

discount n endirim

dishes (kitchen) qab qacaq, boşqablar (mətbəx)

dishwasher qabyuyan maşın

dishwashing liquid qab yumaq üçün maye

display n **(device)** displey (cihazın); **~ case**

disposable n birdəfəlik əşya; **~ razor** birdəfəlik ülgüc

dive v atılmaq

diving equipment dalğıc təchizatı

divorce v boşanmaq

dizzy adj heyrətləndirilmiş

doctor n doktor

doll n kukla

dollar (U.S.) (USD) ABŞ dolları (USD)

domestic yerli; **~ flight** bir ölkənin daxilində reys

door qapı

dormitory yataqxana

double bed ikiqat çarpayı

downtown n şəhərin aşağı hissəsi

dozen djün, kütlə

drag lift ərsin qaldırıcı mexanizmi

dress (clothing) paltar (geyim); **~ code** dress kodu

drink v içmək; **~** n içki; **~ menu** içkilər menyüsu; **~ing water** içməli su

drive v sürmək

driver's license number sürücü vəsiqəsinin nömrəsi

drop n **(medicine)** damcılar (dərman)

drowsiness yuxuculluq

dry clean kimyəvi təmizləmə məruz qoymaq; **~er's** kimyəvi təmizləmə

dubbed təkrar etmək

during müddətdə

duty (tax) rüsum (vergi); **~ free** rüsumla vergi qoyulmaya aid olmayan

DVD rəqəmli kompakt diski

E

ear qulaq; **~ache** qulaqda ağrı

earlier əvvəl

early erkən

earring sırğa

east n şərq

easy rahat

eat v var

economy class iqrtisadi sinif

elbow n dirsək

electric outlet ştepsel rozetkası

elevator lift

e-mail v elektron poçtla göndərmək; **~** n elektron poçt; **~ address** elektron poçtun ünvanı

emergency qəza; **~ exit** ehtiyat çıxışının qapısı

empty v boşaltmaq

end v bitirmək; **~** n son

engaged (person) nişanlanmış (insan)

English adj inglis; **~** n **(language)** ingilis dili

engrave naxış etmək

enjoy həzz almaq

enter v **(place)** girmək (yerə)

entertainment əyləncə

entrance giriş

envelope zərf

epileptic adj epileptik; **~** n epileptik

equipment avadanlıq

escalator eskalator

e-ticket elekton bilet

EU resident Aİ sakini

euro avro

evening n axşam

excess baggage təyin edilmiş normadab artıq baqaj

exchange v mübadilə etmək; **~** n **(place)** mübadilə məntəqəsi (yer); **~ rate** mübadilə kursu

excursion ekskursiya

excuse v bağışlamaq

exhausted tükəldmiş

exit v çıxmaq; **~** n çıxış

expensive qiymətli

experienced təcrübəli

expert ekspert

exposure (film) nümayış (filmin)

express adj təcili; **~ bus** ekspress abtobus; **~ train** ekspress qatar

extension (phone) uzadıcı (telefonun)

extra adj əlavə; **~ large** çox iri

extract v **(tooth)**, çıxartamq, qopartmaq (diş)

eye göz

eyebrow wax qaşlar üçün mum

F

face n üz

facial n üz ifadəsi

family n ailə

fan n **(appliance)** ventilaytor (qurğu)

far (distance) uzaq (məsafə)

farm ferma

far sighted uzaqgörən

fast adj cəld

fat free yağsızlaşdırılmış

father ata

fax v faks üzrə göndərmək; **~** n faks; **~ number** faksın nömrəsi

fee n yığım

feed v yedizdirmək

ferry n keçid

fever n titrətmə

field (sports) meydan (idman)

fill v **(car)** doldurmaq (maşını)

fill out v **(form)** doldurmaq (formanı)

filling n **(tooth)** plomb (diş)

film *n* **(camera)** plyonka (kamerada)

fine *n* **(fee for breaking law)** carima (qanunun puzntusuna görə yığım)

finger *n* barmaq; **~nail** dırnaq

fire *n* yanğın; **~ department** yanğınsöndürən xidməti; **~ door** yanğın çıxışı

first *adj* birinci; **~ class** birinci dərəcəli

fit *n* **(clothing)** əyn (geyim)

fitting room paltarın geyinməsi yeri

fix *v* **(repair)** düzəltmək (təmir etmək)

fixed price menu təsbitlənmiş qiymətlarla menyü

flash photography tutuşma ilə fotoşəkil

flashlight fənərcik

flight *n* uçuş

flip flops nəleyin

floor *n* **(level)** döşəmə (hündürlüyün dərəcəsi)

florist gül alverçisi

flower *n* gül

folk music "faol" stilində musiqi

food ; **~ processor** qida sənayesinin müəssisəsi

foot *n* ayaq

football game [BE] futbal matçı

for barəsində, halında

forecast *n* proqnoz

forest *n* meşə

fork *n* çəngəl

form *n* **(document)** forma (sənəd)

formula (baby) süd qarışığı (uşaqlar üçün)

fort *n* fort

fountain *n* fəvvarə

free *adj* azad

freelance work müqaviləsiz iş, frilans

freezer dondurucu

fresh təzə

friend *n* dost

frozen food dondurunmuş pitsa

frying pan tava

full time *adj* tam iş günü

G

game *n* oyun

garage *n* **(parking)** qaraj (saxlamağı üçün); **~ n (for repairs)** avtoemalatxana (təmir üçün)

garbage bag zibil paketi

gas (car) yanacaq (maşın üçün); **~ station** doldurma

gate (airport) minmə (hava limanında)

gay *adj* **(homosexual)** qey (homoseksual); **~ bar** qeylər barı; **~ club** qeylər klubu

gel *n* **(hair)** gel (saç üçün)

generic drug patentsiz dərman vasitəsi

German *adj* alman; **~ n (language)** alman dili

Germany Almaniya

get off (a train/bus/ subway) düşmək (qatardan/avtobusdan/ metrodan)

gift *n* gədiyyə; **~ shop** hadiyyələr mağazası

girl *n* qız; **~friend** sevgili

give *v* vermək

glass (drinking) stəkan (içməli); **~ (material)** şüşə (material)

glasses eynik

go *v* **(somewhere)** gedmək (harasa)

gold *n* qızıl

golf *n* qalf; **~ course** qolf üçün meydan; **~ tournament** qolf üzrə yarış

good *adj* yaxşı; **~ n** mal; **~ afternoon** gününüz xeyir (gündən sonra); **~ day** ; gününüz xeyir **~ evening** axşamınız xeyir; **~ morning** sabahınız xeyir; **~bye** sağ ol

gram qram

grandchild , nava,nəvə

grandparents baba və nənə

gray *adj* boz

green *adj* yaşıl

grocery store bakaleya mağazası

ground floor kürsülük mərtəbəsi

groundcloth ayaqaltı

group *n* qrup

guide *n* **(book)** rəhbərlik (kitab); **~ n (person)** bələdçi (insan) **~ dog** gəzdirən it

gym *n* **(place)** trenajor zalı (yer)

gynecologist ginekoloq

H

hair saçlar; **~brush** daraq; **~cut** saç qırxma; **~ dryer** saçlar üçün quruducu; **~ salon** bərbərxana; **~ spray** saç üçün lak; **~style** saç düzümü; **~ stylist** saç düzümləri üzrə stilist

halal halal

half *adj* qismən; **~ n** yarı; **~ hour** yarım saat; **~ kilo** yarım kilo

hammer *n* çəkic

hand *n* qol; **~ luggage** əl bağajı; **~ wash** əlyuyan; **~bag [BE]** qadın əl çantası

handicapped əlil; **~ accessible** əlillər üçün təchiz edilmiş

hangover xumarlıq

happy xoşbəxt

hat papaq

have *v* malikolmaq; **~ sex** səxslə məşğul olmaq

hay fever otların çiçəklənməsinə allergiya

head (body part) *n* baş (bədənin hissəsi); **~ache** baş ağrısı; **~phones** baş qarnituması

health sağlamlıq; **~ food store** təbii məhsulların mağazası

hearing impaired pozulmuş eşudma qabiliyyəti ilə

heart ürək; **~ condition** ürəyim vəziyyəti

heat v isitmak; **~er** isitmə cihazı; **~ing** [BE]

hectare hektar

hello salam

helmet dabilqa

help v kömək etmək;**~** n kömək

here burda

hi salam

high hündürda; **~chair** hündür oturacaq; **~lights (hair)** açıq rəngli hissə (saçların); **~way** şosse

hiking boots turist çakmaları

hill n təpə

hire v [BE] (a car) icaraya götürmak (maşını); **~ car** [BE] maşını icaraya götürmak

hockey xokkey

holiday [BE] bayram

horsetrack at hərəkəti üçün yol

hospital xəstəxana

hostel mehmanxana

hot (spicy) acı (ədviyyat haqqında); **~ (temperature)** isti (temperatur); **~ spring** isti bulaq; **~ water** isti su

hotel otel

hour saat

house n ev; **~hold goods** ev üçün mallar; **~keeping services** maişət xidməti

how neca; **~ much** nə qadar

hug v qucqlamaq

hungry ac

hurt v zərər gətirmək

husband ər

I

ibuprofen ibuprofen

ice n buz; **~ hockey** buzüstü xokkey

icy buz bağlanmış

identification eyniləşdirmə

ill xəstə

in içində

include v daxil etmək

indoor pool (public) qapalı hovuz (ictimai)

inexpensive ucuz

infected yoluxdurulmuş

information (phone) soraq xidməti (telefon üzrə); **~ desk** məlumat bürosu

insect haşarat: **~ bite** haşaratın sancması; **~ repellent** haşaratlara qarşı vasitə

insert v (card) salmaq (kartı)

insomnia yuxusuzluq

instant message anı ismarıc

insulin imsulin

insurance sığortalama; **~ card** sığortalama kartı; **~ company** sığorta şirkəti

interesting maraqlı

intermediate orta daracali

international beynəlxalq; **~ flight** beynəlxalq reys; **~ student card** xarici talabanın kartı

internet internet; **~ cafe** internet kafesi;

~ service internet xidmətlər

interpreter tərcüməçi sinxronçu

intersection kəsişmə

intestine bağırsaq

introduce v (person) taqdim etmək (insanı)

invoice n [BE] a hesab faktura

Ireland İrlandiya

Irish adj irland

iron v ütüləmək; **~** n (clothes) ütü

Italian adj italyan

J

jacket n Gödəkçə

Japanese adj yapon

jar n (for jam etc.) banka (mürrabba üçün və s.)

jaw n çana

jazz n jaz; **~ club** jaz klubu

jeans cinslar

jet ski n su xizakları

jeweler zargar

jewelry zərgarlik məmulatları

join v (go with somebody) qoşulmaq (kimləsə getmak)

joint n (body part) oynaq (badanin hissasi)

K

key n açar; **~ card** kart açar; **~ring** açarların bağlaması

kiddie pool uşaqlar üçün hovuz

kidney (body part) böyrak (badanin

hissəsi)

kilo kilo; **~gram** kiloqramm; **~meter** kilometr

kiss v öpmək

kitchen mətbəx; **~ foil** [BE] mətbəx folqası (qol)

knee n diz

knife bıçaq

kosher adj mükəmməl

L

lace n (fabric) krujeva (parçadan)

lactose intolerant laktozanın dözülməzliyi

lake göl

large enli

last adj axırıncı

late (time) gecikmaklə (vaxt)

launderette [BE] özünəxidmətlə camaşırxana

laundromat camaşırxana aparatı

laundry (place) camaşırxana (yer)**~ service** camaşırxana xidmətləri

lawyer n hüquqşunas

leather n dəri

leave v (hotel) oteli tərk etmək; **~ (plane)** tayyarani tərk etmək

left adj, adv (direction), sola, sola (istiqamat)

leg n ayaq

lens linz

less az

lesson n dərs; **take ~s** dərs almaq

letter n maktub
library kitabxana
life jacket xilasedici jilet
lifeguard xilasedici
lift n [BE] lift; **~ n (ride)** lifta gedma; **~ pass** qaldırıcı
light n (cigarette) yandırmaq (siqareti); **~ n (overhead)** işıqlandırmaq; **~bulb** lampa
lighter n alışqan
like v sevmak
line n (train/bus) (/) növba (qatara/ avtobusa)
linen paltar
lip n dodaq
liquor store şarab dükanı
liter litr
little balaca
live v yaşamaq; **~ music** musiqinin canlı yayımı
liver (body part) qaraciyar (badanin hissasi)
loafers mokasinlar
local n (person) yerli (insan)
lock v bağlamaq; **~** n qıfıl
locker şkaf
log off v (computer) sistemdan çıxmaq (kompüter)
log on v (computer) sistema girmak (kompüter)
long adj uzun; **~ sighted** [BE] uzaqgöran; **~ sleeved** uzunqollu

look v baxmaq; **~ for something** naisa axtarmaq
loose (fit) boş (geyim haqqında)
lose v (something) itirmak (naisa)
lost itirmak; **~ and found** itirmak va tapmaq
lotion losyon
louder daha uca
love v (someone) sevmak (kimisa); **~** n sevgi
low aşağı
luggage baqaj; **~ cart** baqajla araba; **~ locker** saxlama kamerası; **~ ticket** baqaj qabzi
lunch n nahar
lung ağciyar (badanin hissasi)
luxury car bağallı maşın

M

machine washable maşın yumasına maslahat görülmüşdür
magazine jurnal
magnificent tamtaraqlı
mail v poçtla göndarmak; **~** n maktab; **~box** poçt qutusu
main attraction proqramın qaymağı
main course öyranmanin asas predmeti
mall ticarat markazi
man (adult male) kişi (yaşlı kişi)
manager menecer

manicure n manikür
manual car mexaniki ötürma qutusuyla minik avtomobili
map n xarita; **~** n (town) şaharin xaritası
market n bazar
married evli, arda
marry evlanmak, ara gedmak
mass n (church service) nahar duası (kilsa xidmati)
massage n massaj
match n kibrit
meal yemak
measure v (someone) ölçmak (kimisa)
measuring cup ölçü fincanı
measuring spoon ölçü qaşığı
mechanic n mexanik
medication (drugs) darman vasitasi (preparat)
medicine darman
medium (steak) orta (steyk)
meet v qarşılamaq
meeting n (business) görüş (biznes); **~ room** görüşlar üçün otaq
membership card iştirakçının kartı
memorial (place) heykal (yer)
memory card yaddaş kartı
mend v (clothes) tikmak (aşyalar)
menstrual cramps menstruasiya spazmaları

menu (restaurant) menyü (restoranda)
message ismarıc
meter n (parking) parkomat; **~** n (measure) ölçü cihazı
microwave mikrodalğalı soba
midday [BE] günorta
midnight gecayarını
mileage millarda masafa
mini bar mini bar
minute daqiqa
missing (not there) yoxluq (burada yoxdur)
mistake n sahv
mobile home takarli ev
mobile phone [BE] mobil telefonu
mobility mobillik
monastery monastır
money pul
month ay
mop n lif süpürga
moped yeyilmiş
more daha çox
morning n sahar
mosque mascid
mother n ana
motion sickness daniz xastaliyi
motor n motor; **~ boat** motorlu qayıq, **~cycle** motosikl, **~way** [BE] avtomobil yolu
mountain dağ; **~ bike** dağ velosipedi
mousse (hair) köpük (saç üçün)
mouth n ağız
movie film; **~ theater** kinoteatr
mug v qarat etmak

multiple trip ticket
bir neçə istifadəylə
gediş bileti
muscle n əzələlər
museum muzey
music musiqi; ~ **store**
musiqi alətlər
mağazası

N

nail file dırnaqlar üçün
mişar
nail salon manikür
salonu
name n ad
napkin salfet
nappy [BE] tüklü
nationality milliyyət
nature preserve
təbiətlə qorunmuş
nausea ürək bulanması
nauseous ürək
bulandırıcı
near yaxın; ~ **sighted**
yaxıngörənlik
nearby yaxında
neck n boyun
necklace boyunbağı
need v möhtac olmaq
newspaper qəzet
newsstand qəzet
kioosku
next adj növbəti
nice xoş
night gecə; ~**club** gecə
klubu
no yox; ~ **(not any)**
heç biri
non alcoholic
alkoqolsuz
non smoking adj siqaret
çəkməyən
noon n günorta
north n şimal
nose burun

note n **[BE] (money)**
qəbz (pul)
nothing heç nə
notify v xəbər vermək
novice yeni
now indi
number n rəqəm
nurse n tibb bacısı

O

office ofis; ~ **hours**
iş saatı
off licence [BE] patent
oil n yağ
OK Okey
old adj köhnə
on the corner küncdə
once (one time) bir vaxt
(bir dəfə)
one bir; **(counting)**
(hesab); ~ **day**
(ticket) birgünlük
(bilet); ~ **way ticket**
(airline) birtərəfli
bilet (təyyarə), **(bus/**
train/subway) (avto-
bus, qatar, metro); ~
way street birtərəfli
istiqamətlə yol
only ancaq ağar
open v açmaq – adj açıq
opera opera; ~ **house**
opera teatrı
opposite n aksilik
optician optik
orange adj **(color)**
narıncı (rəng)
orchestra orkestr
order v **(restaurant)**
sifariş (restorana)
outdoor pool açıq hovuz
outside prep çöldə
over prep **(direction)**
o tərəfə (istiqamət);
~**done (meat)** artıq

yedirtmək (ətlə);
~**heat** v **(car)** artıq
qızdırmaq (maşını);
~**look** n **(scenic**
place)(mənzərəli yer)
seir etmək (; ~**night**
gecə ərzində; ~ **the**
counter (medica-
tion) reseptsiz satılan
(dərman vasitəsi)
oxygen treatment
oksigen terapiyası

P

p.m. günortadan sonra
pacifier sakitləşdirici
vasitə
pack v qablaşdırmaq
package n qablaşdırma
pad n **[BE]** balış
paddling pool [BE]
uşaq üzmə hovuzu
pain ağrı
pajamas pijama
palace saray
pants şalvar
pantyhose kolqotkalar
paper n **(material)** kağız
(material); ~ **towel**
kağız dəsmalı
paracetamol [BE]
parasetamol
park v saxlamaq; ~ n
saxlama; ~**ing garage**
örtülü saxlama
~**ing lot** avtomobil
dayanacağı; ~**ing**
meter parkomat
parliament building
parlament binası
part (for car)
detal (avtomobilin);
~ **time** adj natamam
məşğulluqla
pass through v **(travel)**

keçmək (səyahət)
passenger sərnişin
passport pasport;
~ **control** pasport
nəzarəti
password şifrə
pastry shop şirniyyat
mağazası
patch v **(clothing)**
yamaq (geyim)
path yol
pay v ödəmək; ~**phone**
taksofon
peak n **(of a mountain)**
zirvə (dağın)
pearl n mirvari
pedestrian n piyadaçı
pediatrician pediatr
pedicure n pedikür
pen n qələm
penicillin penisilin
penis penis
perüstündən, ərzində;
~ **day** gün ərzində;
~ **hour** saat ərzində;
~ **night** gecə ərzində;
~ **week** həftə ərzində
perfume n ətir
period (menstrual)
 aylıqlar (aybaşı); ~ **(of**
time) vaxt müddəti
permit n icazə vermək
petrol [BE] yanacaq;
~ **station [BE]**
yanacaqdoldurma
stansiyası
pewter tənəkə
pharmacy əczaçılıq
müəssisəsi
phone v telefonla zəng
etmək; ~ n telefon;
~ **call** telefonla zəng
etmək; ~ **card** telefon
kartı; ~ **number** tel-
efonun nömrəsi

photo foto; **~copy** fotonun surəti; **~graphy** fotoşəkil

pick up v **(person)** pikap, tanış olmaq (insana)

picnic area piknik üçün yer

piece n tika

Pill (birth control) həblər (hamiləliyin qarşısını alan)

pillow n balış

pink adj çəhrayı

piste [BE] cığır; **~ map [BE]** cığırların xəritəsi

pizzeria pitsaxana

place v **(a bet)** malik olmaq, payı etmək

plane n təyyarə

plastic wrap qida plyonkası

plate n boşqab

platform [BE] (train) platforma (vağzalda)

platinum n platin

play v oynamaq; **~** n **(theatre)** tetrda oynamaq; **~ground** oyun meydançası; **~pen** uşaq maneji

please adv buyurun

pleasure n həzz

plunger vantuz

plus size normadan artıq geyim ölçüsü

pocket n cib

poison n zəhər

poles (skiing) xizək çubuğu

police polis; **~ report** polisə ğrizə; **~ station** polis şöbəsi

pond n gölməçə

pool n hovuz

pop music populyar musiqi

portion n porsiya

post n **[BE]** poçt ünvanı; **~ office** poçt şöbəsi; **~ box [BE]** poçt qutusu; **~card** açıqça

pot n dibçək

pottery dulusxana

pound n **(weight)** funt (çəki); **~ (British sterling)** sterlinq funtu (Britaniya valyutası)

pregnant hamilə

prescribe (medication) təyin etmək (dərman vasitəsi)

prescription əmr

press v **(clothing)** ütüləmək (geyimi)

price n qiymət

print v çap etmək; **~** n çap

problem problem

produce n istehsalat; **~ store** istehsalçı mağaza

prohibit qadağan etmək

pronounce bəyan etmək

Protestant protestant

public adj ictimai

pull v dartmaq

purple n bənövşəli

purse n qadın əl çantası

push v sıxmaq; **~chair [BE]** uşaq arabası

Q

quality n keyfiyyət

question n sual

quiet adj sakit

R

racetrack yarış treki

racket n **(sports)** raketka (idmanda)

railway station [BE] dəmityol stansiyası

rain n yağış; **~coat** plaş; **~forest** tropik meşə; **~y** yağışlı

rap n **(music)** rep (musiqi)

rape v zorlamaq; **~** n zorlama

rare nadir

rash n səpgi

ravine dərə

razor blade ülgücün tiyəsi

reach v nail olmaq

ready hazır olmaq

real adj real

receipt n alınma

receive v almaq

reception (hotel) qəbul yeri (oteldə)

recharge v yenidən doldurmaq

recommend tövsiyə etmək

recommendation tövsiyə

recycling takrar istifadə

red adj qırmızı

refrigerator soyuducu

region region

registered mail sifariş poçtu

regular n **(fuel)** requlyar (yanacaq)

relationship münasibətlər

rent v icarəyə almaq; **~** n icarə

rental car icarəyə

götürülmüş avtomobil

repair v təmir etmək

repeat v təkrarlamaq

reservation bron etmək; **~ desk** bron üçün masa

reserve v **(hotel)** bron etmək (oteldə nömrə)

restaurant restoran

restroom ayaqyolu

retired adj **(from work)** istefaya gedən

return v **(something)** qaytarmaq (naisə); **~** n **[BE] (trip)** geriyə yol **reverse** v **(the charges) [BE]** üçün hesabı təqdim etmək

rib n **(body part)** qabırğa (bədənin hissəsi)

right adj, adv **(direction)**, sağ, sağa (istiqamət); **~ of way** gediş haqqı

ring n üzük

river çay

road map yol xəritəsi

rob v qarət etmək

robbed qarətlənmiş

romantic adj romantik

room n otaq; **~ key** otağın açarı; **~ service** nömrələrin xidməti

round trip ikibaşa sayahat

route n yol

rowboat şlyupka

rubbing alcohol tibbi spirt

rubbish n **[BE]** cır cındır; **~ bag [BE]** zibil kisəsi

rugby reqbi

ruin n kəlafəlıq
rush n coşğunluq

s

sad qəmli
safe adj **(protected)** təhlükəsiz (qorunmuş); ~ **(thing)** seyf (əşya)
sales tax satış vergisi
same adj identik
sandals sandal
sanitary napkin gigiyenik salfet
sauna sauna
sauté v yağda qızartmaq
save v **(computer)** saxlamaq (kompüterdə)
savings (account) əmanət (hesabda)
scanner skaner
scarf şərf
schedule v cədvələ daxil etmək; ~ n qrafik
school n məktəb
science elm
scissors qayçı
sea dəniz
seat n oturmaq üçün yer
security mühafizə
see v görmək
self service n özünəxidmət
sell v satmaq
seminar seminar
send v göndərmək
senior citizen yaşlı vətəndaş
separated (person) ayrılmış (insanlar)
serious ciddi
service (in a

restaurant) xidmət (restoranda)
sexually transmitted disease (STD) cinsi əlaqəsi yolu ilə keçən xəstəlik
shampoo n şampun
sharp adj iti
shaving cream təraş üçün krem
sheet n **(bed)** döşəküzü
ship v daşımaq
shirt köynək
shoe store ayaqqabı dükanı
shoe ayaqqabı
shop v almaq; ~ n mağaza
shopping n şopinq; ~ **area** ticarət zonası; ~ **centre [BE]** ticarət mərkəzi; ~ **mall** ticarət mərkəzi
short qısa; ~ **sleeved** qısaqol
shorts şortlar
short sighted [BE] yaxıngörən
shoulder n çiyin
show v göstərmək
shower n **(bath)** duş (vanna otağı)
shrine səcdəgah
sick adj xəstə
side n tərəf; ~ **dish** qarnir; ~ **effect** əlavə təsir; ~ **order** qarnir
sightseeing gərməli yerlərin baxışı; ~ **tour** görməli yerlərin baxışı ilə ekskursiya
sign v **(document)** imzalaq (sənəd)

silk ipək
silver n gümüş
single adj **(person)** tənha (insan); ~ **bed** birnəfərlik çarpayı; ~ **print** yarı çap; ~ **room** birnəfərlik nömrə
sink n balıqqulağı
sister bacı
sit v oturmaq
size n ölçü
ski v xizəkla diyirlənmək; ~ n xizəklər; ~ **lift** dağ xizək qaldırıcı mexanizmi
skin n dəri
skirt n yubka
sleep v yatmaq; ~ **car** yataq vaqonu; ~ **ing bag** yataq kisəsi; ~ **ing car [BE]** yataq vaqonu
slice n tikə
slippers şəp şuplar
slower ləng
slowly asta
small balaca
smoke v siqaret çəkmək
smoking (area) siqaret çəkmək üçün yer
snack bar qəlyanaltı
sneakers kədlər
snowboard n snoubord
snowshoe n xizək
snowy qarlı
soap n sabun
soccer futbol
sock corab
some (with singular nouns) hansısa; ~ **(with plural nouns)** hansılarsa, bir az

soother [BE] əmcək
sore throat boğazda ağrı
south n cənub
souvenir n suvenir; ~ **store** suvenirlər mağazası
spa spa salonu
spatula kürək (kulinaruya)
speak v danışmaq
specialist (doctor) mütəxəssis (həkim)
specimen subyekt
speeding sürətlənmə
spell v hərflər üzrə demak
spicy ədviyyatlarla qatılmış; ~ **(not bland)** acı
spine (body part) kürək (bədənin hissəsi)
spoon n qaşıq
sports idman; ~ **massage** idman massajı
sprain n dartılma
stadium stadion
stairs pilləkən
stamp v **(ticket)** möhürləmək (bilet); ~ n **(postage)** poçt markası
start v başlamaq
starter [BE] başlayan
station n **(stop)** stansiya dayanacaq; **bus** ~ avtobus dayanacağı; **gas** ~ yanacaq doldurma stansiyası; **petrol** ~ **[BE]** yanacaq doldurma stansiyası; **subway** ~ metro stansiyası; **train** ~ dəmiryol stansiyası

statue heykal

steakhouse qalyanaltı

steal v oğurlamaq

steep adj sıldırım

sterling silver sterlinq gümüşü

sting n iynə

stolen oğurlanmış

stomach qarın; ~ache qarında ağrı

stool (bowel movement) oturacaq (defekasiya)

stop v (bus) saxlamaq (avtobus); ~ n (transportation) dayanacaq (nəqliyyat)

store directory (mall) malların kataloqu (ticarət mərkəzində)

storey [BE] qat

stove n plitə

straight adv (direction) düz (istiqamət)

strange təəccüblü

stream n axın

stroller (baby) uşaq arabası

student (university) tələbə (universitetin); ~ (school) məktəb şagirdi

study v oxumaq; ~ing n öyrənmə

stuffed dolğun

stunning dağıdıcı

subtitle v yarımbaşlıq ~ station stansiyanın yarımbaşlığı

suit n kostyum; ~case çamadan

sun n günəş; ~block günəşdən qoruyucu vasitə; ~burn günəş yanığı; ~glasses

günəşdən qoruyan eynəklər; ~ny günəşli; ~screen günəşdən qoruyan ekran; ~stroke gün zərbəsi

super n (fuel) super (yanacaq); ~market supermarket

surfboard serfinq üçün taxta

surgical spirit [BE] tibbi spirt

swallow v udmaq

sweater sviter

sweatshirt svişot

sweet n [BE] şirinlik; ~ adj (taste) şirin (dad)

swelling şiş

swim v udmaq; ~suit çimmə kostyumu

symbol (keyboard) simvol (klaviaturada)

synagogue sinaqoq

T

table n masa

tablet (medicine) həb

take v, qəbul etmək, götürmək

tampon n tampon

taste v (test) dadına baxmaq

taxi n taksi

team n komanda

teaspoon çay qaşığı

telephone n telefon

temple (religious) qala (dini)

temporary müvəqqəti

tennis tennis

tent n tent; ~ peg çadır üçün paya; ~ pole çadır üçün dirək

terminal n (airport)

terminal (hava limanı)

terrible dəhşətli

text v (send a message) mesajları yazmaq; ~ n mətn

thank v təşəkkür etmək; ~ you sizə təşəkkür edirəm

the bu, həminki

theater teatr

theft oğurluq

there burada

thief oğru

thigh bud

thirsty susuzluğa məruz qalan

this bu, əsl, verilən

throat boğaz

thunderstorm tufan

ticket n bilet; ~ office bilet kassası

tie n (clothing) qalstuk (geyim)

tight (fit) dar (geyim haqqında)

tights [BE] triko

time vaxt; ~table [BE] (transportation) cədvəl (marşrutların)

tire n şin

tired yorğun

tissue parça

tobacconist tütün məmulatların alverçisi

today adv bu gün

toe n ayağın barmağı

toenail ayağın barmağındakı dırnaq

toilet [BE] ayaqyolu; ~ paper tualet kağızı

tomorrow adv sabah

tongue n dil

tonight bu gün axşam

to (direction) harasa,

harasa

tooth diş

toothpaste diş macunu

total n (amount) cəmi (say)

tough adj (food) bərk (yemək haqqında)

tour n tur

tourist turist; ~ information office turistik bürosu

tow truck dartıcı

towel n dəsmal

tower n qala

town n şəhər; ~ hall şəhər məclisi; ~ map şəhərin xəritəsi; ~ square şəhər meydanı

toy oyuncaq; ~ store oyuncaqlar dükanı

track n (train) dəmiryol yolları

traditional ənənəvi

traffic light işıqfor

trail n (ski) cığır; ~ map cığırlar xəritəsi

trailer (car) treyler (maşın)

train n qatar; ~ station dəmiryol stansiyası

transfer v (change trains/flights) dəyişmək (reysi/qatarı dəyişmək); ~ (money) pulları köçürmək

translate tərcümə etmək

trash n zibil

travel v səyahət etmək; ~ agency turizm şirkəti; ~ sickness yırğalama; ~ers check [cheque BE] yol qəbzi tree ağac

trim (hair) v qırxmaq (saçları)

trip n turistik yürüş

trolley [BE] (grocery store) araba (ərzaq dükanı); ~ [BE] (luggage) baqaj arabası

trousers [BE] şalvar

T shirt futbolka

tumble dry qurudma

turn off v (device) söndürmək (cihaz)

turn on v (device) yandırmaq (cihaz)

TV Yeleviziya

tyre [BE] avtomobil şini

U

ugly eybəcər

umbrella çətir

unbranded medication [BE] damğasız dərman vasitəsi

unconscious (faint) Halsızlıq

underdone yarımçıq görülmüş

underground n [BE] metro; ~ station [BE] metro stansiyası

underpants [BE] tumanlar

understand v başa düşmək

underwear alt paltarı

United Kingdom (U.K.) Böyek Britaniya

United States (U.S.) ABŞ

university universitet

unleaded (gas)

etillaşməmiş (yanacaq)

upset stomach mədənin hazm edilməməsi

urgent təcili

urine sidik

use v istifadə etmək

username istifadəçinin adı

utensil qab

V

vacancy (room) boş yer (sahə)

vacation çazuniyyət

vaccination peyvandlanma

vacuum cleaner tozsoran

vaginal infection vaginal infeksiya

valid qüvvədə olan

valley vadi

valuable adj qiymətli

value n dəyər

van furqon

VAT [BE] ƏDV

vegan n veqan; ~ adj veqan

vegetarian n vegetarian; ~ adj vegetarian

vehicle registra-tion avtomobilin qeydiyyatı

viewpoint (scenic) [BE] icmal nöqtəsi (mənzərəli)

village kənd

vineyard üzümlük

visa viza

visit v baş çəkmək; ~ing hours baç çəkmə saatları

visually impaired zəif görən

vitamin vitamin

V neck V hərfi formasında yaxanın kəsiyi

volleyball game voleybol oyunu

vomit v qusmaq; ~ing qusuntu

W

wait v gözləmək; ~ n gözləmə

waiter ofisiant

waiting room gözləmə otağı

waitress ofisiant qız

wake v yuxudan durmaq; ~ up call zəng zəngli saat

walk v gedmək; ~ n yeriş; ~ing route piyada marşrutu

wallet pul kisəsi

war memorial müharibə qurbanları heykəli

warm v (something) qızdırmaq (nəisə); ~ adj (temperature) iliq temperatur

washing machine paltaryuyan maşın

watch v baxmaq

waterfall şəlalə

wax v (hair) mum (saçlar üçün)

weather n hava

week həftə; ~end istirahət günləri

weekly hər həftə

welcome adj qabul; you're ~ nuş olsun

west n şimal

what nə

wheelchair əlil

arabası; ~ ramp əlil arabaların düşməsi üçün pandus

when adv (at what time) nə vaxt (hansı müddətdə)

where harada

white adj ağ; ~ gold ağ qızıl

who (question) kim (sual)

widowed dul qalmış

wife arvad

window pancarə; ~ case vitrin

wine list şərab kartı

wireless simsiz; ~ phone simsiz telefon

with

withdraw v (money) hesabdan vasitələri çıxartmaq; ~al (bank) hesabların çıxardılması

without olmadığı halda

woman qadın

wool yun

work v işləmək

wrap v bükmək

wrist bilak

write v yzamaq

Y

year il

yellow adj sarı

yes bəli

yesterday adv dünən

young adj cavan

youth hostel gənclər turist bazası

Z

zoo zoopark

AZERBAIJANI–ENGLISH

A

ABŞ dolları (USD) dollar (U.S.)
ABŞ United States (U.S.)
ac hungry
acı (ədviyyat haqqında) hot (spicy); **isti (temperatur)** ~ (temperature); **isti bulaq** ~ spring; **isti su** ~ water
açar key n; **kart-açar** ~ card; **açarların bağlaması** ~ring
açıq hovuz outdoor pool
açmaq open v; **açıq** ~ adj
ad günü birthday
ad name n
adapter adapter
ağ white adj; **ağ qızıl** ~ gold
ağac tree
ağciyar (bədənin hissəsi) lung
ağız mouth n
ağrı pain
axın stream n
axırıncı last adj
axşam evening n
Aİ sakini EU resident
ailə family n
akupunktura acupuncture
agentlik agency
alçaq low adj
alınma receipt n
alışqan lighter n
alkoqolsuz non-alcoholic

allergik allergic; **allergik reaksiya** ~ reaction
almaq buy v
almaq receive v
almaq shop v; **mağaza** ~ n
alman German adj; **alman dili** ~ n (language)
Almaniya Germany
almaz diamond
alt paltarı underwear
alt tumanı (geyim) briefs (clothing)
alternativ yol alternate route
alüminium folqası aluminum foil
amerikanlı American adj
ana mother n
ancq agar only
anesteziya anesthesia
anı ismarıc instant message
antibiotik antibiotic n
antiseptik krem antiseptic cream
appendiks (bədənin hissəsi) appendix (body part)
araba (ərzaq dükanı) trolley [BE] (grocery store); **baqaj arabası** ~ [BE] (luggage)
araba (ərzaq dükanından) cart (grocery store); **baqaj arabası** ~ (luggage)
aradan qaldırmaq (kompüter) delete v (computer)

arxada (istiqamət) behind (direction)
arkada arcade
aromaterapiya aromatherapy
arteriya artery
artrit arthritis
arvad wife
asiyalı Asian adj
aspirin aspirin
asta slowly
astmatik asthmatic
at hərəkəti üçün yol horsetrack
ata father
atılmaq dive
avadanlıq equipment
Avro euro
Avstraliya attractive
avstraliyalı Australian adj
avtobus bus n; **avtobus stansiyası** ~ station; **avtobus dayanacağı** ~ stop; **avtobusda gediş üçün bilet** ~ ticket; **avtobusda tur** ~ tour
avtomatik automatic; **avtomatik maşın** ~ car
avtomobil şini tyre [BE]
avtomobilin qeydiyyatı vehicle registration
ay month
ayağın barmağı toe n
ayağın barmağındaki dırnaq toenail
ayaq foot n
ayaq leg n
ayaqaltı groundcloth

ayaqqabı dükanı shoe store
ayaqqabı shoe
ayaqyolu restaurant
ayaqyolu toilet [BE]; **tualet kağızı** ~ paper
ayırmaq (kompüteri) disconnect (computer)
aylıqlar (aybaşı) period (menstrual); **vaxt müddəti** ~ (of time)
ayrılmış (insanlar) separated (person)
az less
azad free adj
azqanlı anemic

B

baba və nənə grandparents
bacı sister
bağalı maşın luxury car
bağırsaq intestine
bağışlamaq excuse v
bağlamaq (mağaza) close v (a shop)
bağlamaq lock v; **qıfıl** ~ n
bağlıdır closed
baxış (maşının) breakdown (car)
baxmaq look v; **nəisə axtarmaq** ~ for something
baxmaq watch v
bakaleya mağazası grocery store
baqaj baggage [BE]; **baqajın verilməsi** ~ claim; **baqaj qəbzi** ~ ticket

baqaj qəbzi ~ ticket
baqaj qəbzi check in
(luggage); **nə isə**
yoxlamaq ~ (on
something)
baqaj luggage; **baqajla**
araba ~ cart
balaca little
balaca small
balet ballet
balıqqulağı sink *n*
balış pad *n* [BE]
balış pillow *n*
bank bank *n*
banka (mürəbbə
üçün və s.) jar *n* (for
jam etc.)
bankomat ATM;
bankomat üçün kart
~ card
bankomat kartı ATM ~;
kredit kartı credit ~;
debet kartı debit ~;
telefon kartı phone ~
bar (yer) bar (place)
barbekü (qurğu-
barbekü üçün qril)
barbecue (device) *n*
barəsində, halında for
barmaq finger *n*dırnaq
~nail
basketbol basketball
baş (bədənin hissəsi)
head (body part) *n*;
baş ağrısı ~ache
baş çəkmək visit *v*; **baç**
çəkmə saatları ~ing
hours
baş qarniturası
~phones
başa düşmək under-
stand *v*
başlamaq begin
başlamaq start *v*
başlayan beginner

başlayan starter [BE]
batareya battery
bayram holiday [BE]
bazar market *n*
bej beige *adj*
beynəlxalq interna-
tional; **beynəlxalq**
reys ~ flight;
xarici tələbənin
kartı ~ student card
beysbol baseball
bəli yes
bənövşəli purple *adj*
bərbər barber
bərk (yemək haqqında)
tough *adj* (food)
bəyan etmək pronounce
bıçaq knife
bikini bikini
bilet ticket *n*; **bilet**
kassası ~ office
biləк wrist
bina building
biotualet chemical toilet
bir neçə istifadəylə
gediş bileti multiple-
trip ticket
bir one; (hesab)
(counting); **birgünlük**
(bilet) ~-day (ticket);
birtərəfli bilet
(təyyarə) ~-way ticket
(airline), (avtobus, qa-
tar, metro) (bus/train/
subway); **birtərəfli**
istiqamətlə yol
~-way street
bir ölkənin daxilində
reys flight
bir vaxt (bir dəfə) once
(one time)
birdəfəlik əşya
disposable
birdəfəlik ülgüc razor
birinci ~ door ; birinci

dərəcəli ~ class
birləşmək (internet)
connect (internet)
bitirmək end *v*,son ~ *n*
biznes business *adj*;
biznes kartı ~ card;
biznes mərkəz
~ center; **biznes sinif**
~ class; **iş saatları**
~ hours
blender blender
boğaz throat
boğazda ağrı sore throat
boks matçı boxing
match
bort board *v*; **minmə**
talonu ~ing pass
boş (geyim haqqında)
loose (fit)
boş yer (sahə) vacancy
(room)
boşaltmaq empty *v*
boşanmaq divorce *v*
boşqab plate *n*
botanik bağ botanical
garden
boyun neck *n*
boyunbağı necklace
boz grandparents
böcək (həşərat) bug
(insect) *n*
Böyek Britaniya United
Kingdom (U.K.)
böyrək (bədənin
hissəsi) kidney (body
part)
böyük big; **artıq** ~ger
britaniyalı British *adj*
bron etmək (oteldə
nömrə) reserve *v*
(hotel)
bron etmək reservation;
bron üçün masa
~ desk
bu gün axşam tonight

bu gün today *adv*
bu, əsl, verilən this
bu, həminki the
bud thigh
burada there
buraxılış access *n*
burda here
burğu corkscrew *n*
burun nose
butulka bottle *n*;
butulkaları açmaq
üçün quğu ~ opener
buz bağlanmış ~ hockey
buz ice *n*; **buzüstü**
xokkey ~ hockey
bükmək wrap *v*
büllür (şüşə) crystal *n*
(glass)

C

cari hesab current
account [BE]
cavan young *adj*
cədvələ daxil etmək
schedule *v*; **qrafik** ~ *n*
cəlb etmə (yer üzrə)
attraction (place)
cəlbedici attractive
cəld fast *adj*
cəmi (say) total *n*
(amount)
cənub south *n*
cərimə (qanunun
puzntusuna görə
yığım) fine *n* (fee for
breaking law)
cib pocket *n*
ciddi serious
cığır piste [BE];
çığırların xəritəsi
~ map [BE]
cığır trail *n*
(ski); **cığırlar**
xəritəsi~ map

cihaz accommodation
cinsi əlaqəsi yolu ilə keçən xəstəlik sexually transmitted disease (STD)
cinslər jeans
cır cındır rubbish *n* [BE]; **zibil kisəsi ~** bag [BE]
corab sock
coşğunluq rush *n*

Ç

çamaşırxana (yer) laundry (place); **çamaşırxana xidmətləri** – service; **hüquqşunas** lawyer *n*; **dəri** leather *n*
çamaşırxana aparatı laundromat
çanta ~pack
çanta bag
çap etmək print *v*; **çap ~** *n*
çay qaşığı teaspoon
çay river
çəhrayı pink *adj*
çəkic hammer *n*
çəkmə boot *n*
çənə jaw *n*
çəngəl fork *n*
çətir umbrella
çəzuniyyat vacation
çıxartmaq, qopartmaq (diş) extract *v* (tooth)
çıxmaq exit *v*; **çıxış ~** *n*
çimərlik beach
çin Chinese *adj*
çirkin dirty
çirklənmiş constipated
çiyin shoulder *n*
çöldə outside *prep*
çörək dükanı bakery

D

dadına baxmaq taste *v* (test)
dadlı delicious
dağ mountain; **dağ velosipedi** ~ bike
dağıdıcı stunning
daha çox more
daha uca louder
daha yaxşı better
daxil etmək include *v*
dalğıc təchizatı diving equipment
damcılar (dərman) drop *n* (medicine)
damğasız dərman vasitəsi unbranded medication [BE]
danışmaq speak *v*
dantist dentist
dar (geyim haqqında) tight (fit)
daraq comb *n*
darıxdırıcı boring
dartıcı tow truck
dartılma sprain *n*
dartmaq pull *v*
daşımaq ship *v*
dayə ~sitter
debet kartı debit card
detal (avtomobilin) part (for car); **natamam məşğulluqla ~** time *adj*
dezodorant deodorant
dəbilqə helmet
dəhşətli terrible
dəqiqə minute
dəmiryol yolları track *n* (train)
dəmiryol stansiyası railway station [BE]
dəniz xəstəliyi motion sickness ; **motor** motor *n*; **motorlu qayıq** ~ boat; **motosikl** ~cycle; **avtomobil yolu** ~way [BE]
dəniz sea
dərə ravine
dərəcə (temperatur) degree (temperature)
dəri skin *n*
dərin deep *adj*
dərman medicine
dərman vasitəsi (preparat) medication (drugs)
dərs lesson *n*; **dərs almaq** take ~s
dəsmal towel *n*
dayar value *n*
dəyişmək (reysi/qatarı dəyişmək) transfer *v* (change trains/flights); **pulları köçürmək ~** (money)
dəyişmək (uşaq bezi) change *v* (baby) **avtobusa minmək**(~ (buses); **pulları dəyişmək ~** (money); **sdəç (pul) ~** *n* (money)
dəyişmək alter *v*
diabetik diabetic *adj*; **diabetik** diabetic
dibçək pot *n*
dil tongue *n*
dırnaqlar üçün mişar nail file
dirsək elbow *n*
displey (cihazın) display (device)
diş məcunu toothpaste
diş protezləməsi denture
diş tooth
diz knee *n*
dizel yanacağı diese

djün, kütlə dozen
dodaq lip *n*
doktor doctor *n*
doldurmaq (formanı) fill out *v* (form)
doldurmaq (maşını) fill *v* (car)
dolğun stuffed
dondurucu freezer
dondurunmuş pitsa frozen food
dost friend
döş breast; **əmizdirmək ~feed** *v*
döşəküzü sheet *n* (bed)
döşəmə (hündürlüyün dərəcəsi) floor *n* (level)
döyüş meydanı battleground
dress-kodu dress-code
dul qalmış widowed
dulusxana pottery
durğunluq (orqanizmdə) congestion (medical)
duş (vanna otağı) shower *n* (bath)
dünən yesterday *adv*
düşərgə camp *n*; **yürüş sobası ~ing** stove; **düşərgənin yerləşməsi ~site**
düşmək (qatardan/ avtobusdan/metrodan) get off (a train/ bus/subway)
düz (istiqamət) straight *adv* (direction)
düzaltmaq (təmir etmək) fix *v* (repair)

E

ekskursiya excursion
ekspert expert

elekton bilet e-ticket
elektron poçtla göndərmək e-mail v; **elektron poçt** ~ n; **elektron poçtun ünvanı** ~ address
elm science
endirim discount
enli large
epileptik epileptic adj **epileptik** ~n
erkən early
eskalator escalator
etilləşmamiş (yanacaq) unleaded (gas)
ev house n; **ev üçün mallar** ~hold goods; **məişət xidməti** ~keeping services
evlənmək, ərə gedmək marry
evli, ərdə married
eybəcər tyre [BE]
eynək glasses
eyniləşdirmə ~ hockey

ə

əczaçılıq müəssisəsi pharmacy
ƏDV VAT [BE]
ədviyyatlarla qatılmış spicy; acı ~ (not bland)
əksilik opposite n
əl yükü (əl baqajı) carry-on n (piece of hand luggage)
əlaqə (səyahatlar/internet) connection (travel/internet); **birləşma reysi** ~ flight
əlaqəyə girmək contact v
əlavə dəyər cover charge

əlavə extra adj; **çox iri** ~ large
əlçatan available
əlil arabası wheelchair; **əlil arabanın düşməsi üçün pandus** ~ ramp
əlil handicapped; **əlillər üçün tachiz edilmiş** ~-accessible
əlillərə əlçatan accessible [BE]
əmanət (hesabda) savings (account)
əmcək soother [BE]
əmr prescription
ən yaxşısı best adj; **yaxşısı_ qabaq istifadə etmək** ~ before
ənənəvi traditional
ər husband
ərsin qaldırıcı mexanizmi drag lift
ətir perfume n
əvvəl before
əvvəl earlier
əyləncə entertainment
əyləncə parkı amusement park
əyn (geyim) fit n (clothing)
əzələlər muscle n
əziz cute

F

faks üzrə göndərmək fax v; **faks** ~ n; **faksın nömrəsi** ~ number
faol stilində musiqi folk music
ferma farm
fənərcik flashlight
fəvvarə fountain n
film movie; **kinoteatr**

~ theater
fincan cup n
forma (sənəd) form n (document)
fort fort
foto photo; **fotonun surəti** ~copy; **fotoşəkil** ~graphy
fotoplyonkanı etmək develop v (film)
funikulyor cable car
funt (çəki) pound n (weight); **sterlinq funtu (Britaniya valyutası)** ~ (British sterling)
furqon van
futbal matçı football game [BE]
futbol soccer
futbolka T shirt

G

gecə night; **gecə klubu** ~club
gecəyarısı midnight
gecikdirmək delay v
gecikməklə (vaxt) late (time)
gedmək (harasa) go v (somewhere)
gedmək walk v; **yeriş** ~ n; **piyada marşrutu** ~ing route
gel (saç üçün) gel n (hair)
geyim clothing; **geyim mağazası** ~ store
gədiyyə gift n; **hədiyyələr mağazası** ~ shop
gələm pen n
gəlmə arrival
gəlmək arrive
gəlmək come v

gənclər turist bazası youth hostel
gərməli yerlərin baxışı sightseeing; **görməli yerlərin baxışı ilə ekskursiya** ~ tour
gətirmək bring
gəzdirən it ~ dog
gigiyenik salfet sanitary napkin
ginekoloq gynecologist
giriş entrance
giriş qiyməti (qiymət) admission (price)
girmək (yerə) enter v (place)
gödəkçə jacket n
göl lake
gölməçə pond n
gömrük nəzarəti customs
gömrükdə əşyaları təqdim etmək declare v (customs)
göndərmək send v
görmək see v
görüş (biznes) meeting n (business); **görüşlər üçün otaq** ~ room
göstərmək show v
göy blue adj
göz eye
gözəl beautiful; **çarpayı** ~ bed n; **çarpayı və səhər yeməyi** ~ and breakfast
gözləmə otağı waiting room
gözləmək wait v; **gözləmə** ~ n
gül alverçisi florist
gül flower n
gümüş silver n
gün day

günəş sun n; günəşdən
qoruyucu vasita
~block; günəş yanığı
~burn; günəşdən
qoruyan eynəklər
~glasses; günəşli
~ny; günəşdən
qoruyan ekran
~screen; gün zərbəsi
~stroke

günorta midday [BE]

günorta noon n

günortadan sonra p.m.

H

hadisə accident

halal halal

halsızlıq unconscious
(faint)

hamilə pregnant

hansısa some (with
singular nouns);
hansılarsa, bir az
~ (with plural nouns)

harada where

harasa, harasa to
(direction)

hava air n;
havanın kon-
disiyalaşdırılması
~ conditioning; quru
havalı ~dry; hava
pompası ~ pump;
avia xətt ~line;
aviapoçt ~mail;
təyyarə ~plane; hava
limanı ~port

hava weather n

hazır olmaq ready

hazırlamaq cook v

heç biri ~ (not any)

heç nə nothing

hektar hectare

hesab (bank hesabı)
account n (bank)

hesab (pul) bill n
(money); qəbz ~ (of
sale)

hesabdan vasitələri
çıxartmaq;withdraw
v (money) hesabların
çıxardılması ~al
(bank)

hesab-faktura invoice
n [BE]

heykəl (yer) memorial
(place)

heykəl statue

heyrətləndirilmiş
dizzy adj

heyvan animal

həb tablet (medicine)

həblər (hamiləliyin
qarşısını alan) Pill
(birth control)

həftə week; istirahət
günləri ~end

həlalik bye

həmkar colleague

hər həftə weekly

hərflər üzrə demək
spell v

həzz almaq enjoy

həzz pleasure n

hovuz pool n

hücum etmək attack v

hündürdə high; hündür
oturacaq ~chair;
açıq rəngli hissə
(saçların) ~lights
(hair); şosse ~way

X

xəbər vermək notify v

xərclər cost v

xəritə map n; şəhərin
xəritəsi ~ n (town)

xəstə ill

xəstə sick adj

xəstəxana hospital

xidmət (restoranda)
service (in a
restaurant)

xilasedici jilet life
jacket

xilasedici lifeguard

xizək çubuğu poles
(skiing)

xizək snowshoe n

xizəklə diyirlənmək
ski v; xizəklər ~ n;
dağ xizak qaldırıcı
mexanizmi ~ lift

xokkey hockey

xoş nice

xoşbəxt happy

xumarlıq hangover

ibuprofen ibuprofen

icarəyə almaq rent v;
icarə ~ n

icarəyə götürmək
(maşını) hire v [BE] (a
car);maşını icarəyə
götürmək ~ car [BE]

icarəyə götürülmüş
avtomobil rental car

icazə vermək allow

icazə vermək permit v

icəsənət art

iclas zalı convention hall

icmal nöqtəsi
(mənzərəli) viewpoint
(scenic) [BE]

ictimai public adj

içində in

içkilər menyusu
~ menu

içmək drink v; içki~;
içməli su ~ing water

identik same adj

idman sports; dman
massajı ~ massage

ikibaşa səyahət

round trip

ikiqat çarpayı double
bed

iqrtisadi sinif economy
class

il year

imsulin insulin

imzalaq (sənəd) sign v
(document)

indi now

inglis English adj; ingilis
dili ~ n (language)

internet internet; in-
ternet kafesi ~ cafe;
internet xidmətlər
~ service

ipək silk

İrland Irish adj

İrlandiya Ireland

ishal diarrhea

isitmək heat v;
isitmə cihazı ~er;
нагревание ~ing [BE]

ismarıc message

istefaya gedən retired
adj (from work)

istehsalat produce n;
istehsalçı mağaza
~ store

istifadə etmək use v

istifadəçinin adı
username

istiqamət direction

iş saatı ~ hours

işıqfor traffic light

işləmək qabiliyyətini
itirmiş (əlil) disabled
adj (person)

işləmək work v

iştirakçının kartı
membership card

italyan Italian adj

iti sharp adj

itirmək (nəisə) lose v
(something)

itirmək lost; **itirmək və tapmaq** ~-and-found
iynə sting n

J

jaz jazz n; **jaz klubu** ~ club
jurnal magazine

K

kabare cabaret
kafe (yer) cafe (place)
kağız (material) paper n (material); **kağız dəsmalı** ~ towel
kalafalıq ruin n
kaloriya calorie
kamera camera; **kameranın çexolu** ~ case; **rəqəmli kamera** digital ~
Kanada Canada
kanadalı Canadian adj
kanyon canyon
kar deaf adj
kart card n
kasa bowl n
kassadar cashier
kazino casino
keçid aisle; **keçiddə yer** ~ seat
keçid ferry n
keçmək (səyahət) pass through v (travel)
kedlər sneakers
keyfiyyət quality n
kənd village
kəsişmə intersection
kəsmək cut v; **kəsik (yara)** ~ n (injury)
kibrit match n
kilo kilo; **kiloqramm** ~gram; **kilometr** ~meter
kilsə cathedral

kilsə church
kim (sual) who (question)
kimyəçi chemist [BE]
kimyəvi təmizləmə məruz qoymaq dry clean; **kimyəvi təmizləmə** ~er's
kişi (yaşlı kişi) man (adult male)
kitab book n; **kitab mağazası** ~store
kitabxana library
klassik musiqi classical music
klub club n
kolqotkalar pantyhose
komanda team n
kompüter computer
konfet candy
konfrans conference
konsert concert; **konsert zalı** ~ hall
konserv bankalarının açılması üçün qurğu can opener
konservləşdirilmiş məhsul canned good
konsulluq consulate
kontakt linzaları contact lens; **kontakt linzaları üçün məhlul** ~ solution
konveyer xətti conveyor belt
kostyum suit n; **çamadan** ~case
köhnə old adj
kömək etmək help v; **kömək** ~ n
köpük (saç üçün) mousse (hair)
körpü bridge
köynək blouse
köynək shirt

kredit kartı credit card
krem (maz) cream (ointment)
krujeva (parçadan) lace n (fabric)
kukla doll n
küncdə on the corner
kürək (bədənin hissəsi) back (body part)
kürək (bədənin hissəsi) spine (body part)
kürək (kulinaruya) spatula
kürəkdə ağrı ~ache
kürsülük mərtəbəsi ground floor

Q

qab utensil
qab yumaq üçün maye dishwashing liquid
qabırğa (bədənin hissəsi) rib n (body part)
qab-qacaq, boşqablar (mətbəx) dishes (kitchen)
qablaşdırma package n
qablaşdırmaq pack v
qabyuyan maşın dishwasher
qadağan etmək prohibit
qadın əl çantası purse n
qadın woman
qala (dini) temple (religious)
qala tower n
qalf golf n; **üçün meydan** ~ course; **qolf üzrə yarış** ~ tournament

qalstuk (geyim) tie n (clothing)
qan axmaq bleed
qan blood; **qan təzyiqi** ~ pressure
qapalı hovuz (ictimai) indoor pool (public)
qapı door
qara black adj
qaraciyər (bədənin hissəsi) liver (body part)
qaraj (saxlamaq üçün) garage n (parking); **avtoemalatxana (təmir üçün)** ~ n (for repairs)
qardaş brother
qarət etmək mug v
qarət etmək rob v
qarətlənmiş robbed
qarın stomach; **qarında ağrı** ~ache
qarlı snowy
qarşılamaq meet v
qastronomiya mağazası delicatessen
qaşıq spoon n
qaşlar üçün mum eyebrow wax
qat storey [BE]
qatar train n; **dəmiryol stansiyası** ~ station
qayıcı scissors
qayıq boat n
qayış belt
qaynadmaq boil v
qaytarmaq (nəisə) return v (something); **üçün hesabı təqdim etmək** ~ [BE] (trip) **qabırğa (bədənin hissəsi)** reverse v (the charges) [BE]

qey (homoseksual)
gay *adj* (homoseksual);
qeylər barı ~ bar;
qeylər klubu ~ club
qəbul etmək accept *v*
qəbul etmək,
götürmək take *v*
qəbul etməmək (kredit
kartını) decline *v*
(credit card)
qəbul welcome *adj*; **nuş**
olsun you're ~
qəbul yeri (oteldə)
reception (hotel)
qəbz (ödəniş üzrə) *n*
(payment); **yoxlama**
~-in; **hesabı yox-**
lamaq ~ing account;
baxmaq ~-out
qəbz (pul) note *n* [BE]
(money)
qəhvayi brown *adj*
qəlyanaltı appetizer
qəlyanaltı snack bar
qəlyanaltı steakhouse
qəmli sad
qəssab butcher *n*
qəza emergency; **ehtiyat**
çıxışının qapısı ~ exit
qəzet kiosku newsstand
qəzet newspaper
QİCS AIDS
qida plyonkası plastic
wrap
qıfıl castle
qırxmaq (saçları) trim
(hair) *n*
qırma (soymaq
maqsədi ilə) break-in
(burglary) *n*
qırmızı red *adj*
qısa short; **qısaqol** ~-
sleeved
qismən half *adj*; **yarı**
~ *n*; **yarım saat**

~ hour; **yarım kilo**
~-kilo
qiymət price *n*
qiymətli valuable *adj*
qız girl; **sevgili** ~friend
qızdırmaq (nəisə) warm
v (something); **ilıq**
temperatur ~ *adj*
(temperature)
qızıl gold *n*
qol (bədənin hissəsi)
arm *n* (body part)
qol hand *n*; **əl baqajı**
~ luggage; **əlyuyan**
~ wash; **qadın əl**
çantası ~-bag [BE]
qolbaq bracelet
qoşulmaq (kiminsə
getmək) join *v* (go
with somebody)
qoymaq (pulları)
deposit *v* (money);
banka əmanət ~ *n*
(bank)
qrafin carafe
qram gram
qrup group *n*
qucqlamaq hug *v*
qulaq ear
qulaqda ağrı ~ache
qurudma tumble dry
qusmaq vomit *v*;
qusuntu ~ing
quş bird
qüvvədə olan valid
qyimətli expensive

L

laktozanın
dözülməzliyi lactose
intolerant
lağv cancel
ləng slower
lif süpürgə mop *n*
lifçik bra

lift elevator
lift lift *n* [BE]; **getmə**
~ *n* (ride); **qaldırıcı**
~ pass
linz lens
litr liter
losyon lotion

M

mağara cave *n*
malik olmaq, payı
etmək place *v* (a bet)
malikolmaq have *v*;
sexslə məşğul
olmaq ~ sex
malların kataloqu
(ticarət mərkəzində)
store directory (mall)
manikür manicure *n*
manikür salonu nail
salon
maraqlı interesting
masa table *n*
massaj massage *n*
maşın car; **maşını**
sifariş etmək
~ hire [BE]; **maşını**
saxlamaq ~ park
[BE]; **maşını icarəyə**
götürmək ~ rental;
maşının oturacaq
~ seat
mehmanxana hostel
mexanik mechanic *n*
mexaniki ötürmə
qutusuyla minik
avtomobili manual
car
menecer manager
menstruasiya
spazmaları menstrual
cramps
menyü (restoranda)
menu (restaurant)
mesajları yazmaq text

v (send a message);
mətn ~ *n*
meşə forest *n*
metro underground *n* [BE];
metro stansiyası
~ station [BE]
meydan (idman) field
(sports)
mədənin həzm
edilməməsi upset
stomach
məktəb school *n*
məktub letter *n*
mənzil apartment
məscid mosque
maslahət görülmüşdür
machine washable
məsləhətçi consultant
mətbəx, ~ foil [BE]
mətbəx folqası (qol)
mikrodalğalı soba
microwave *n*
millərdə məsafə
mileage
milliyyət nationality
mini bar mini-bar
minmə (hava
limanında) gate
(airport)
mirvari pearl *n*
mis copper *n*
mobil telefonu cell
phone
mobil telefonu mobile
phone [BE]
mobillik mobility
mokasinlər loafers
monastır monastery
möcüzəli amazing
möhtac olmaq need *v*
möhürləmək (bilet)
stamp *v* (ticket); **poçt**
markası ~ *n* (postage)
mum (saçlar üçün) wax
v (hair)

musiqi music; **musiqi alatlər mağazası** ~ store

muzey museum

mübadilə etmək exchange v; **mübadilə məntəqəsi (yer)** ~ n (place); **mübadilə kursu** ~ rate

müddətdə during

mühafizə security

müharibə qurbanları heykəli war memorial

mükəmməl kosher adj

müqaviləsiz iş, frilans freelance work

münasibətlər relationship

mürəkkəb difficult

mütəxəssis (həkim) specialist (doctor)

müvəqqəti temporary

N

nadir rare

nahar dinner

nahar duası (kilsə xidməti) mass n (church service)

nahar lunch n

naxış etmək engrave

nail olmaq reach v

narahat olmaq bother v

narıncı (rəng) orange adj (color)

neca how; **nə qədər** ~ much

nə vaxt (hansı müddətdə) when adv (at what time)

nə what

nəfəs almaq breathe

naleyin flip-flops

nəvə,nəvə grandchild

nişanlanmış (insan) engaged (person)

normadan artıq geyim ölçüsü plus size

nömrəni yığmaq dial v

növbə(qatara/avtobusa) line n (train/bus)

növbəti next adj

nümayiş (filmin) exposure (film)

O

o tərəfə (istiqamət) over prep (direction);

artıq yedirtmək (ətlə) ~done (meat);

artıq qızdırmaq (maşını) ~heat v (car); **(mənzərəli yer)-sehr etmək** ~look n (scenic place);

gecə ərzində ~night;

reseptsiz satılan (dərman vasitəsi) ~-the-counter (medication)

odekolon cologne

ofis office

ofisiant qız waitress

ofisiant waiter

oğlan boy; **dost** ~friend

oğru thief

oğurlamaq steal v

oğurlanmış stolen

oğurluq theft

oxumaq study v; **öyrənmə** ~ing n

Okey OK

oksigen terapiyası oxygen treatment

olmadığı halda without, **olmaq** be v

opera opera; **opera teatrı** ~ house

optik optician

orkestr orchestra

orta (steyk) medium (steak)

orta dərəcəli intermediate

otaq room n; **otağın açarı** ~ key; **nömrələrin xidməti** ~ service

otel hotel

oteli tərk etmək leave v (hotel); **təyyarəni tərk etmək** ~ plane)

otların çiçəklənməsinə allergiya hay fever

oturacaq (defekasiya) stool (bowel movement)

oturacaq chair n; **asma qaldırıcısı** ~ lift

oturmaq sit v

oturmaq üçün yer seat n

oynaq (bədənin hissəsi) joint n (body part)

oynamaq play v; **tetrda oyanmaq** ~ n (theatre); **oyun meydançası** ~ground; **uşaq manejı** ~pen

oyun game n

oyuncaq toy; **oyuncaqlar dükanı** ~ store

ödəmək pay v; **taksofon** ~phone

ödəniş (kredit kartdan) charge v (credit card); **ödənişin dəyəri** ~ (cost)

ölçmək (kimisa) measure v (someone)

ölçü fincanı measuring cup

ölçü qaşığı measuring spoon

ölçü size n

ölkənin kodu country code

öpmək kiss v

örtük coat

öskürmək cough v; **öskürək** ~ n

öyrənmənin əsas predmeti main course

özünəxidmət self service n

özünəxidmətlə camaşırxana launderette [BE]

P

paltar (geyim) dress (clothing)

paltar linen

paltarın geyinməsi yeri fitting room

paltaryuyan maşın washing machine

pambıq cotton

pambıq parça denim

papaq hat

parasetamol paracetamol [BE]

parça tissue

parkomat meter n (parking); **ölçü cihazı** ~ n (measure)

parlament binası parliament building

pasport passport; **pasport nəzarəti** ~ control

patent off-licence [BE]

patentsiz dərman vasitəsi generic drug

pediatr pediatrician

pedikür pedicure n

penis penis

penisilin penicillin

peyvəndlanma vaccination

pəncərə window; vitrin
~ case
pijama pajamas
pikap tanış olmaq
(insanla) pick up v
(person)
piknik üçün yer picnic
area
pilləkən stairs
pitsaxana pizzeria
piyadaçı pedestrian
platforma (vağzalda)
platform [BE] (train)
platin platinum n
plita stove n
plomb (diş) filling n
(tooth)
plyonka (kamerada)
film n (camera)
poçt ünvanı post n [BE];
poçt şöbəsi ~ office;
poçt qutusu ~box
[BE]; açıqca ~card
poçtla göndərmək mail
v; məktəb ~ n; poçt
qutusu ~box
polis police; polisə
ğrizə ~ report; polis
şöbəsi ~ station
populyar musiqi pop
music
porsiya portion n
pozulmuş eşidmə
qabiliyyəti ilə hearing
impaired
prezervativ condom
problem problem
proqnoz forecast n
proqramın qaymağı
main attraction
protestant Protestant
pul cash n;
ödəmək ~ v
pul kisəsi wallet
pul money

R

rahat easy
raketka (idmanda)
racket n (sports)
real real adj
region region
reqbi rugby
requlyar (yanacaq)
regular n (fuel)
rep (musiqi) rap n
(music)
restoran restaurant
rəhbərlik (kitab) guide
n (book); bələdçi
(insan) ~ n (person)
rəqəm number n
rəqəmli digital; rəqəmli
kamera ~ camera;
rəqəmli fotoşəkil
~ photo; rəqəmli çap
~ print
rəqəmli kompakt-
diski DVD
rəqs etmək dance v;
rəqs klubu ~ club;
rəqs edən ~ing
rəng color n
romantik romantic adj
rüsum (vergi) duty (tax)
rüsuma vergi qoyul-
maya aid olmayan
~-free

S

saat hour
sabah tomorrow adv
sabun soap n
saçlar hair; daraq
~brush; saç qırxma
~cut; saçlar üçün
qurucu ~ dryer;
barbarxana ~ salon;
saç üçün lak ~spray;
saç düzümü ~style;
saç düzümləri üzrə

stilist ~ stylist
saçlara qulluq üçün
vasitə conditioner
(hair)
sağ, sağa (istiqamət)
right adj, adv (direc-
tion); gediş haqqı
~ of way
Sağlam olasız Cheers!
sağlamlıq health;
təbii məhsulların
mağazası ~ food store
saxlama kamerası
~ locker
saxlamaq (avtobus)
stop v (bus); dayana-
caq (nəqliyyat) ~ n
(transportation)
saxlamaq
(kompüterdə) save v
(computer)
saxlamaq park v;
saxlama ~ n; örtülü
saxlama ~ing
garage; avtomobil
dayanacağı ~ing lot;
parkomat ~ing meter
sakit quiet adj
sakitləşdirici vasitə
pacifier
saqqız chewing gum
salam hello
salam hi
salfet napkin
salmaq (kartı) insert
v (card)
sancaq brooch
sandal sandals
Santimetr centimeter
saray palace
sarğı bandage
sarı yellow adj
satış vergisi sales tax
satmaq sell v
sauna sauna

SD diski CD
Selsi dərəcəsi Celsius
seminar sell v
serfinq üçün taxta
surfboard
Sertifikat certificate
sevmək (kimsə) love
v (someone); sevgi ~ n
sevmək like v
səbət (ərzaq
dükanında) basket
(grocery store)
səcdəgah shrine
səhər morning n
səhər yeməyi
breakfast n
səhra desert n
səhv mistake n
səpgi rash n
sərin (temperatur) cool
adj (temperature)
sərnişin passenger
səyahət etmək travel
n; turizm şirkəti
~ agency; yırğalama
~ sickness; yol qəbzi
~ers check (cheque
BE)
sidik kisəsi bladder
sidik sidik urine
sifariş (restoranda)
order v (restaurant)
sifariş poçtu registered
mail
sığortalama insurance;
sığortalama kartı
~ card; sığorta
şirkəti ~ company
sıxmaq push v; uşaq
arabası ~chair [BE]
sikkə coin
siqara cigar
siqaret çəkmək smoke v
siqaret çəkmək üçün
yer smoking (area)

siqaret çəkməyən non-smoking *adj*

siqaret paçkası carton (of cigarettes); **ərzaqlar üçün karton paketi** ~ (of groceries);

sıldırım qaya cliff

sıldırım steep *adj*

silmək (bankomatda daxil etmək üçün satir) clear *v* (on an ATM)

simsiz wireless; **simsiz telefon** ~ phone

simvol (klaviaturada) symbol (keyboard)

sinaqoq synagogue

sındırmaq (sümüyü) break *v* (bone)

sinə (bədənin hissəsi) chest (body part); **sinədə ağrı** ~ pain

sinif class *n*; **biznes sinifi** business ~; **ekonom sinif** economy ~; **birinci sinif** first ~

sınmış broken

sınmış sümük ~ (bone)

sırğa earring

sistemdən çıxmaq (kompüter) log off *v* (computer)

sistemə girmək (kompüter) log on *v* (computer)

skaner scanner

snoubord snowboard *n*

sola, sola (istiqamət) left *adj*, (direction) *adv*

sonra after; **günorta** ~noon; **təraş** ~shave

soraq xidməti (telefon üzrə) information

(phone); **məlumat bürosu** haşarat ~ desk; insect: **həşaratın sancması** ~ bite; **həşaratlara qarşı vasitə** ~ repellent

soyuducu refrigerator

soyuqdəymə (xəstəlik) cold *n* (sickness); **soyuq (temperatur)** ~ *adj* (temperature)

söndürmək (cihaz) turn off *v* (device)

spa salonu spa

srücü vəsiqəsinin nömrəsi driver's license number

stadion stadium

stansiya dayanacaq station *n* (stop); **avtobus dayanacağı** bus ~; **yanacaq doldurma stansiyası** gas ~; **yanacaq doldurma stansiyası** petrol ~ [BE]; **metro stansiyası** subway ~; **dəmiryol stansiyası** train ~

sterlinq gümüşü sterling silver

stəkan (içməli) glass (drinking); **şüşə (material)** ~ (material)

su xizəkləri jet ski *n*

sual question *n*

subyekt specimen

super (yanacaq) super *n* (fuel); **supermarket** ~market

susuzluğa məruz qalan thirsty

suvenir mağazası antiques store

suvenir souvenir *n*; **suvenirlər mağazası** ~ store

süd qarışığı (uşaqlar üçün) formula (baby)

sümük bone *n*

süpürgə broom

sürətlənmə speeding

sürmək drive *v*

süzgəc colander

svişot sweatshirt

sviter sweater

Ş

şalvar pants

şalvar trousers [BE]

şampun shampoo *n*

şəp şuplar slippers

şezlonq deck chair

şəhər town; **şəhər məclisi** ~ hall; **şəhərin xəritəsi** ~ map; **şəhər meydanı** ~ square **şəhərin aşağı hissəsi** downtown *n*

şəlalə waterfall

şərab dükanı liquor store

şərab kartı wine list

şərf scarf

şərq east *n*

şifrə password

şikayət complaint

şimal north *n*

şimal west *n*

şin tire *n*

şirinlik sweet *n* [BE];

şirin (dad) ~ *adj* (taste)

şirniyyat mağazası pastry shop

şiş swelling

şkaf locker

şlyupka rowboat

şopinq shopping *n*;

ticarət zonası ~ area; **ticarət mərkəzi** ~ centre [BE]; **ticarət mərkəzi** ~ mall

şortlar shorts

ştepsel rozetkası electric outlet

T

taksi taxi *n*

tam iş günü full-time *adj*

tampon tampon *n*

tarix (təqvim) date *n* (calendar)

tava frying pan

teatr theater

telefon telephone *n*

telefonla zəng etmək phone *v*; **telefon** ~ *n*; **telefonla zəng etmək** ~ call; **telefon kartı** ~ card; **telefonun nömrəsi** ~ number

tennis tennis

tent tent *n*; **çadır üçün paya** ~ peg; **çadır üçün dirək** ~ pole

terminal (hava limanı) terminal *n* (airport)

təbiətlə qorunmuş nature preserve

təcili express *adj*; **ekspress abtobus** ~ bus; **ekspress qatar** ~ train

təcili urgent

təcili yardım ambulance

təcrübəli experienced

təəcüblü strange

təhlükəli dangerous

təhlükəsiz (qorunmuş) safe *adj* (protected); **seyf (əşya)** ~ *n* (thing)

tək (tənhalıqda) alone
təkərli ev mobile home
təkrar etmək dubbed
təkrar istifadə recycling
təkrarlamaq repeat v
təqdim etmək (insanı)
  introduce v (person)
tələbə (universitetin)
  student (univer-
  sity); **məktəb şagirdi**
  ~ (school)
təmir etmək repair v
təmizləmək clean
  v; ~ adj **təmiz**
  (geyim) (clothes);
  təmizləmək üçün
  məhsul ~ing product
təmizləyən vasitə
  detergent
təmtəraqlı magnificent
tənəkə pewter
tənha (insan) single adj
  (person); **birnəfərlik**
  çarpayı ~ bed;
  yarı çap ~ print;
  birnəfərlik nömrə
  ~ room
təpə hill n
təraş üçün krem shav-
  ing cream
tərcümə etmək
  translate
tərcüməçi-sinxronçu
  interpreter
tərəf side n; **qarnir**
  ~ dish; **əlavə təsir**
  ~ dish; **qarnir** ~ order
təsbitlənmiş
  quymətlarla menyü
  fixed-price menu
təsdiq etmək confirm
təşəkkür etmək thank
  v; **sizə təşəkkür**
  edirəm ~ you
təyin edilmiş nor-

madab artıq baqaj
  excess baggage
təyin etmək (dərman
  vasitəni) prescribe
  (medication)
təyinat appointment
təyyarə plane n
təzə fresh
tibb bacısı nurse n
tibbi spirt rubbing
  alcohol
tibbi spirt surgical
  spirit [BE]
ticarət mərkəzi mall
tikə piece n
tikə slice n
tikmək (əşyaları) mend
  v (clothes)
titrətmə fever n
topuq ankle
tormoz (maşında)
  brake (car)
tormoz brake v
tozsoran vacuum
  cleaner
tövsiyə etmək recom-
  mend
tövsiyə recommendation
trenajor zalı (yer) gym
  n (place)
treyler (maşın) trailer
  (car)
triko tights [BE]
tufan thunderstorm
tumanlar underpants
  [BE]
tur tour n
turist çəkmələri hiking
  boots
turist tourist; **turistik**
  bürosu ~ information
  office
turistik yürüş trip n
tutuşma ilə fotoşəkil
  flash photography

tükəldilmiş exhausted
tüklü nappy [BE]
tünd dark adj
tütün məmulatların
  alvercisi
  tobacconist

U

ucuz cheap; **daha**
  ucuz ~er
ucuz inexpensive
uçuş (təyyarə)
  departure (plane)
uçuş flight n
udmaq swallow v
univermaq department
  store
universitet university
unlanmış breaded
uşaq arabası stroller
  (baby)
uşaq baby; **uşaq**
  bezi diaper; **uşaq**
  butulkası ~ bottle;
  uşaq çarpayısı crib
uşaq kreslosu child ;
  ~'s seat
uşaq menyüsü
  children's menu
uşaq porsiyası
  children's portion
uşaq salfetləri ~ wipe
uşaq üzmə hovuzu
  paddling pool [BE]
uşaqlar üçün hovuz
  kiddie pool
uzadıcı (telefonun)
  extension (phone)
uzaq (məsafə) far
  (distance)
uzaqgörən far-sighted
uzun long adj;
  uzaqgörən ~-sighted
  [BE]; **uzunqollu**
  ~-sleeved

Ü

ülgücün tiyəsi razor
  blade
ünvan address n
ürək bulandırıcı
  nauseous
ürək bulanması
  nausea
ürək heart; **ürəyim**
  vəziyyəti ~ condition
üstündən, ərzində per;
  gün ərzində ~ day;
  saat ərzində ~ hour;
  gecə ərzində ~ night;
  həftə ərzində ~ week
ütüləmək (geyimi)
  press v (clothes)
ütüləmək iron v; **ütü** ~ n
  (clothes)
üz face n
üz ifadəsi facial n
üzmək swim v; **çimmə**
  kostyumu ~suit
üzük ring n
üzümlük vineyard

V

V hərfi formasında
  yaxının kəsiyi V neck
vadi valley
vaginal infeksiya
  vaginal infection
vaxt time; **cədval**
  (marşrutların) ~table
  [BE] (transportation)
valyuta currency;
  valyuta mübadiləsi
  ~ exchange; **valyuta**
  mübadilə məntəqəsi
  ~ exchange office
vanna otağı bathroom
vantuz plunger
var eat v
vegetarian vegetarian n;
  vegetarian ~ adj

veqan vegan n; **veqan ~** adj
velosiped bicycle
velosiped yolu bike route
velosipedda getma cycling
ventilaytor (qurğu) fan n (appliance)
vermak give v
vaziyyat (sahhatin) condition (medical)
vilayatin kodu area code
vitamin vitamin
viza visa
voleybol oyunu volleyball game

Y

yaddaş kartı memory card
yağ oil n
yağda qızartmaq sauté v
yağış rain n; **plaş ~coat;** **tropik meşa ~forest;** **yağışlı ~y**
yağsızlaşdırılmış fat free
yaxın near; **yaxıngöranlik ~-sighted**
yaxında (küncün arxasında) around (the corner); **taxmini qiymat ~** (price)
yaxında nearby
yaxıngöran short sighted [BE]

yaxşı good adj; **mal ~** n; **gününüz xeyir (gündan sonra) ~** afternoon; **gününüz xeyir ~** day; **~** evening **axşamınız xeyir; sabahınız xeyir ~** morning; **sağ ol ~**bye
yamaq (geyim) patch v (clothing)
yan buttocks
yanacaq (maşın üçün) gas (car); **doldurma ~** station
yanacaq petrol [BE]; **yanacaqdoldurma stansiyası ~** station [BE]
yandırmaq (cihaz) turn on v (device)
yandırmaq (siqareti) light n (cigarette); **işıqlandırmaq ~** n (overhead); **lampa ~**bulb
yandırmaq burn v
yanğın fire n **yanğınsöndüran xidmati ~** department; **yanğın çıxışı ~** door
yapışqan qaysaq cling film [BE]
yapon Japanese adj
yarımbaşlıq subtitle n; **stansiyanın yarımbaşlığı ~** station
yarımçıq görülmüş

underdone
yarış treki racetrack
yaş age n
yaşamaq live v; **musiqinin canlı yayımı ~** music
yaşıl green adj
yaşlı vatandaş senior citizen
yataqxana dormitory
yatmaq sleep v; **yataq vaqonu ~er car; yataq kisasi ~ing bag; yataq vaqonu ~ing car** [BE]
yedizdirmak feed v
Yeleviziya TV
yemak food; **qida sanayesinin müəssisasi ~** processor
yemak meal
yemak üçün çöplar chopsticks
yemakxana dining room
yeni novice
yenidan doldurmaq recharge v
yerli domestic
yerli (insan) local n (person)
yeyilmiş moped
yığım fee n
yox no
yoxluq (burada yoxdur) missing (not there)
yol xaritasi road map
yol path
yol route n

yoluxdurulmuş inexpensive
yoluxucu contagious
yorğan blanket
yorğun tired
yubka skirt n
yuxuculluq drowsiness
yuxudan durmaq wake v; **zang zangli saat ~** up call
yuxusuzluq insomnia
yumru kasik crew neck
yun wool
yüngül bland
yzamaq write v

Z

zadalamak damage v
zahar poison n
zahg vurmaq (telefonla) call v (phone); **çağırmaq ~** n; **abunaçinin hesabına zang vurmaq ~** collect
zaif göran visually impaired
zara gatirmak hurt v
zarf envelope
zargar jeweler
zargarlik mamulatları jewelry
zibil paketi garbage bag
zibil trash n
zirva (dağın) peak n (of a mountain)
zoopark zoo n
zorlamaq rape v; **zorlama ~** n

INDEX

pocket guide

BAKU

First Edition 2020

Editor: Sian Marsh
Author: Farida Zeynalova
Head of DTP and Pre-Press: Rebeka Davies
Managing Editor: Carine Tracanelli
Picture Editor: Aude Vauconsant
Layout: Agnieszka Bylica
Cartography: Carte
Photography Credits: Alamy 23, 65, 70; AWL
Images 1; Getty Images 15, 19, 20, 26, 83, 85,
93; iStockphoto 4MC, 4ML, 4TL, 4TC, 5M, 5T,
5TC, 5MC, 5MC, 5M, 6L, 6R, 7, 7R, 11, 13, 25,
28, 32, 35, 36, 39, 40, 45, 47, 48, 49, 50, 55,
58, 60, 63, 67, 73, 74, 75, 77, 86, 88, 90, 96,
101, 102, 107; Shutterstock 17, 24, 30, 43, 53,
57, 68, 79, 81, 84, 94, 105
Cover Picture: Shutterstock

Distribution
UK, Ireland and Europe: Apa Publications
(UK) Ltd; sales@insightguides.com
United States and Canada: Ingram
Publisher Services; ips@ingramcontent.com
Australia and New Zealand: Woodslane;
info@woodslane.com.au
Southeast Asia: Apa Publications (SN) Pte;
singaporeoffice@insightguides.com
Worldwide: Apa Publications (UK) Ltd;
sales@insightguides.com

**Special Sales, Content Licensing
and CoPublishing**
Insight Guides can be purchased in bulk
quantities at discounted prices. We can
create special editions, personalised jackets
and corporate imprints tailored to your
needs. sales@insightguides.com;
www.insightguides.biz

Contact us
Every effort has been made to provide
accurate information in this publication,
but changes are inevitable. The publisher
cannot be responsible for any resulting loss,
inconvenience or injury. We would appreciate
it if readers would call our attention to any
errors or outdated information. We also
welcome your suggestions; please contact
us at: berlitz@apaguide.co.uk
www.insightguides.com/berlitz

Baku Metro